Another Slice of Paradise

Share Sandra and Steve's ongoing experiences at their rustic horse farm in the Mountains of Portugal.

A sequel to Sandra's first book *Paradise*

CONTENTS

ACKNOWLEDGEMENTS

I would like to thank my very good friend Sue Clarkson for all her help and encouragement, and also for her beautiful paintings which adorn both of my books. She is a very talented lady.

Also huge thanks to Innokentij Kreknin for the typesetting of the paperback.

And this facebook group is a real gem for memoir authors and everyone who loves this genre.

www.facebook.com/groups/welovememoirs/

INTRODUCTION

My first book, titled "*Paradise*" tells of our journey from Brighton, England, to a new life in the mountains of Portugal, and how fate led us to Paradise...a derelict, dirt floored ruin on the banks of a crystal clear Portuguese mountain river. Along with me on the journey were Steve, my wonderful resourceful husband, Craig, our nine year old son, our dog Toby, a 7 year old Labrador type mongrel and our three horses. We were enchanted at first sight by the stunning location of the ruin. It was surrounded by trees, and so quiet apart from the birds singing and the burble of the river. But the ruin had no electricity, running water, or telephone connection. There were no services at all. It was to be the biggest challenge of our lives, we were stepping back 100 years time, living with candle and gas lighting, and carrying water up from our mountain spring.

It's been an amazing experience to breathe life back into the crumbling walls of our ruin. Steve and I are both proud to have done it, and in fact we are still doing it to this day!

Another big part of my story is horses; they have always been my passion. We brought our three horses from England with us and started offering horse riding holidays. This added a whole different adventure to our lives, and within a year, we had seven horses, three dogs, three cats, and three chickens. Over the next few years, two beautiful foals were born at our farm; all of these animals have enriched our lives and have etched their own characters into our story.

Our son Craig was only nine years old at the time, we were amazed at the way he overcame some huge obstacles; like starting at a Portuguese school, where nobody spoke English. We have had some great adventures, and some tough times, but I have loved every minute of it.

I hope you enjoy sharing our ongoing story in my second book titled "*Another Slice of Paradise.*" This takes in the next 12 years of our life in Portugal, from the end of 1999 to 2012. Many guests visit our little corner of Paradise to ride our horses and see for themselves the stunning beauty of the Portuguese countryside. You will meet new people, horses, dogs, and fowl, as well as catching up with the older animals, and hopefully learning a little more about Portugal and its wonderful friendly people. Our dream to build a lovely little guest cottage becomes a reality, and a surprise encounter leads to us building our own riding arena.

Our life seems to be a rollercoaster of happiness and heartbreak, but our old house and the river below are our constant.

I am always happy to receive emails at *sandracross421@gmail.com*

I also have a Facebook page, where I am constantly uploading photos of our farm and the animals that you will meet in my books:

https://www.facebook.com/SandraCross421

CHAPTER 1

SERIOUS NEGOTIATIONS

"Ouch! What was that?" I looked down at my leg as jaws closed around my flesh. A primal panic convulsed through me, and I just managed to stifle a guttural scream. I froze as I focused on what was wriggling under the weight of my foot: I was treading on the tail of a huge thick green/brown snake, and it was rearing up for a second attack, spitting at me in anger. Steve instantaneously turned around and pushed me off its tail, and the serpent slithered away, seemingly unhurt, into the dense undergrowth. Steve cupped my leg in his hands and studied the bite mark.

"I don't think it was venomous, but I'd better take you to the clinic to get it checked out."

It had obviously shaken him up as much as it had me, I could feel the tremor in his hands. There were tiny spots of blood starting to appear on my leg in a circle of teeth marks, but no deeper fang marks. I could picture the face of the snake and still see its gaping mouth and flicking forked tongue. The teeth had all been small, with no fangs that I could see, and its eyes had been wide, not slit, as they are in most poisonous snakes. It had a beautiful greenish body that was more than a metre long.

"It had probably been sunbathing across the track, still sleepy from hibernation and basking in the warmth." Steve surmised as he studied my leg. "It certainly had a rude awakening" he added. "I saw it, but through my sunglasses it looked like a branch lying

1

across the track and I just stepped over it. Its camouflage worked too well for its own good!"

I had been too close behind him, and had landed right on the poor creature's tail!

"I'm sure I will be ok, I will tell you immediately if I feel strange in any way. I don't want to go to the clinic, let's just go home," I pleaded earnestly.

We made our way back across the weir which dammed the river, and stopped to gaze up at our beautiful old house. We still couldn't believe how lucky we were to have found it, even after living in it for almost five years. We had bought it as a ruin and it had continuously emptied our pockets ever since. When we had first arrived in Portugal, searching for a quieter, more natural existence, it seemed as though fate was leading us to this ruin on the banks of a beautiful river. It stood in solitude, completely surrounded by nature; the only sounds were the burbling of the river and the birdsong. The old ruin had looked daunting, but the surroundings were magical, and we both instinctively knew that we had found our own little piece of paradise.

We were young and had plenty of energy and optimism, which we had needed ceaselessly during our first five years. Our initial sighting of the old, seemingly abandoned barn had changed our lives forever. There had been no electricity or any water supply; it was just a draughty old barn with no glass in the windows and gaping holes in the upper wooden floor. The lower floor was just dirt, and would have housed animals in the past; the smell of them still lingered in the air.

Yet we had been thrilled by the sheer diversity of the terrain. Two ancient olive trees stood near the barn, and majestic cork oak trees interspersed with pines and eucalyptus surrounded the perimeter. Wild roses and ivy clambered up the walls, and an old orange tree stood in the middle of the yard, its boughs heavy with uneaten fruit. The rushing sound of the river was always present as it cascaded over a weir below us. Frogs serenaded in full voice, and cicadas ceaselessly rubbed their back legs to announce their presence in the high eucalyptus trees, making a sound that I always associate with warm summer days. Two mature fig trees, one black and one green, stood like sentries on the border, the tiny figs were already formed; just waiting for a full summer of sunshine to swell and ripen them. It truly was a magical place.

Eventually, we had become the proud (or should that be mad!) owners. Most of the renovations on the barn had been done by Steve, my wonderful resourceful husband, and we had a fantastic group of friends that we had met since moving here, who were always on hand whenever we needed a bit more muscle. Swapping labour was still commonplace; Steve often helped out neighbours and they would do the same for him. Our latest project, after five years of gas lighting and candles, was to install a meagre solar installation. This would give us a very basic electricity supply for the first time in five years, and for the house, the first time ever! Solar power, at this time, was still in its infancy in Portugal and therefore expensive. The unit that we were installing would only supply us with a few lights, music and some hot water for showers.

We were also in the process of buying some land next to our house with a ruin standing on it which was literally four crumbling walls. The plot was owned by twelve different people! Eleven of the owners of this small plot of land, were due to arrive at our house shortly to walk the boundaries, which was the reason I didn't want to waste time going to the clinic after my encounter with 'William Snakespeare'. I was feeling fine and I had no ill effects at all; I just hoped the poor snake was ok.

Steve had baked some small cakes and biscuits, and had bought a 'chouriço' and some goat's cheese from our neighbour Francisco, who was one of the owners of the ruin. His wife Maria had baked us some of her special onion broa bread that she knew we loved. Broa bread has a high maize content and lands like a brick in your stomach, but it's very tasty, especially with a bit of onion thrown into the mixture. We had laid out a mini feast, which was the tradition when serious negotiations were taking place. Of course, there would also be wine!

There was a feud between the eleven owners and the twelfth owner. Antonio totally refused to be present to walk the boundaries, and instead he had come the day before by himself, to walk the land with us. He warned us constantly to beware of the other owners, and to remember the boundaries that he was showing us as they would try to cheat us out of land. He was the only one to be trusted, the others were little more than criminals in his eyes. They had been stealing the land of his forefathers for centuries he told us, from under bushy furrowed eyebrows.

We had taken his warnings with a pinch of salt and were looking forward to the afternoon's negotiations. Most of the owners were from our neighbouring village, and they all walked along to our house together. One man lived further away and as we listened, we heard the 'pop, pop, splutter' of his old Zundapp motorbike. Five minutes later he finally pulled up and took off his helmet: sound travels on these winding mountain roads!

We knew our neighbours on first name terms, so after much air kissing and back slapping, we got down to the job in hand— walking the land. It was an L shaped plot, with some forest on the other side of the road, probably about one third of an acre in all. The ruin was just four crumbling mud walls which had fallen down due to an earthquake in the 1970's. One of our neighbours told us the history of the land while we enjoyed a glass of wine and a tasty treat. He said that there had been two cottages on the plot, but one had fallen completely and was now just rubble. The cottages had been homes for labourers working on a big farm which was about 300 metres from us. The farm had fallen on hard times during the civil war and along with our house, had been requisitioned by the army. He told us that our house had been under siege, which would explain the bullet shaped holes in our ancient front door. We had always wondered what had made those holes but would never have guessed that our lovely old house sitting so peacefully in nature was once a war zone!

Before and after the war, our house had been the caretaker's house where numerous families had lived for hundreds of years. They would have lived on the first floor with their animals living underneath them. Our old neighbour told us that his grandmother had inherited the house from her parents, and he had been born under its roof. In those times the upper floor, which is now our lovely spacious lounge room, was split into seven rooms where his whole family cooked, ate and slept. There was no sanitation or water or electricity, yet he had lived in this house with his grandparents, his parents and his brothers, and stabled below the wooden floor were twenty goats and a pig. When we had first bought the house, part of a wall had been black with soot from the fire that would have burned there. We scraped it all off and painted it white, but after a winter of rain and damp, the black was seeping back through, so we had to do a better job and scrape it all back to rock, then render the whole wall, before painting it again.

Our lovely veranda, which was now bedecked with a table for outdoor eating, hammocks, and many plants, had not been a place for relaxation...there was no time for that; it had been full of bee hives. It would have been a very basic lifestyle which changed little through the centuries. But in the 1970s, an earthquake shook the foundations of our house, causing a cavernous crack to run from the roof downwards, and the petrified inhabitants had fled for their lives never to return.

Our house had then stood empty for about 20 years; the roof was caving in and one wall of the house was badly cracked and threatening to crumble. At some time there had been a fire that burned down the veranda. It wouldn't have taken many more years before the round river boulders, from which the house was built, would have found their way back into the river. These old houses made of river boulders and mud didn't last for long once the roof caved in and the rain washed the mud away.

Luckily for us and our house, a young English guy called Adam had literally stumbled on it and had started the huge job of renovating it. He and a friend bought the ruin between them, and set about basic renovations. They strengthened the crumbling wall, and using all of the old oak beams and original tiles, they had re-roofed the whole house. His dream was to bring his girlfriend out to Portugal and raise a family in this wonderful natural environment. Sadly for him, but not for us, his girlfriend didn't want to leave her beloved Scotland, so we had been lucky enough to buy the old house, which had never had electricity, running water, or any other modern necessities.

Eduardo was the village elder, if I wanted to find out more about the history of our house, he would be the one to ask, but now was not the right time.

Steve brought out the piece of paper given to him by our feuding neighbour Antonio, and passed it to Eduardo, asking him if he agreed with the boundaries that Antonio had written down. He nodded in agreement.

"Sim, tudo correto" he said as he handed it to the second man, who nodded enthusiastically. He then handed it to the next person, who was also nodding in agreement with the other two, when suddenly a young female voice shouted in Portuguese from the back of the crowd.

"It's no good showing it to any of them...none of them can read." A nervous titter arose before Eduardo explained to us that very few of the mountain people of his era had gone to school. There was no public transport and the school was too far to walk; also children were expected to help their parents with farm work so there was no time for school. Our neighbours may not have been able to read, but they had a wealth of knowledge about the life cycle of the land, crops, and seasons. They were all very friendly; I couldn't imagine that the things Antonio had said about them could possibly be true. I think that old feuds get dramatised over the generations, but life is too short and we wanted to be friends with all of our neighbours...even Antonio!

A few weeks later, we were the proud owners of a piece of scrub land and a few piles of rocks which just about resembled the walls of a dwelling. We moved our chickens into the walls for safety at night from foxes, and that was how it stayed for the next couple of years as we carried on with renovating our own house and building our growing horse-riding empire!

We had brought our three horses with us from England, the first was a very boisterous troublemaker called Roxy. He was a beautiful bright bay Welsh cob, but don't ever be fooled by his cute face, dear reader; he was a monster, but I loved him with all of my heart, although he drove me to despair in many a situation. For instance, one day I set out for a ride with two guests riding Guv and Smartie, (my other two horses) and me riding Roxy. Guv was leading, but he stopped and refused to go forward. This was not like him, so I jumped off Roxy, and led him to the front to see what the problem was. There were the remains of a dead sheep on the path. Horses don't like to cross dead things, so I tried to lead Roxy away from the path, hoping Guv and Smartie would follow me. Roxy reared up, and snatching the reins out of my hand, galloped off into a meadow of grass. I led Guv and Smartie away from the sheep and onto a patch of grass, and told their riders to let them eat grass while I went to catch Roxy. As soon as I approached him, he galloped off again, his mouth full of grass; it was as if he were laughing at me. This happened two more times; I shouted at him through tears of frustration and humiliation, before deciding that the safety of my riders was my paramount concern. I turned my back on him and stomped back to the group, drying my eyes and trying to get a grip on my anger. I think he realised that he had overstepped the line, and I became aware of his presence as he trotted up behind me with a cute, innocent expression on his face. He followed meekly behind me back to the group, and stood still while I mounted, which was not like him at all. He behaved perfectly for the rest of the ride: my loveable rogue!

Guv was a bay Irish thoroughbred; my dependable, reliable, loyal partner. I called him my partner because I trusted him completely and he never let me down. When things didn't go to plan on a ride...which, believe me happened... I could always rely on him to see us through. For instance, we had ridden through freak thunder/hail storms, limbs crashing down from trees precariously close to us in the forests, marching bands and village festivals, practising fighter jets flying ridiculously low, being threatened by herds of wild pigs, the list was endless, but Guv just marched on through (as long as there were no dead animals!) Roxy and Smartie would follow him anywhere, they trusted him too.

Smartie was a spirited grey Arab, very kind and a great favourite with our customers. He had a flowing silky white mane, and his tail flew proud and high like a flag in high wind. He was a real beauty and very clever. If his rider was experienced, he could fly like the wind, but if his rider were a novice, he would be quiet and kind. I could write a book on the clever antics of this super little horse, and maybe one day I will!

He was also the favourite horse of our son Craig, who had been just 9 years old when we first arrived in Portugal, and who was now a young bi-lingual teenager of 13. He had settled really well at school, considering he couldn't speak a word of Portuguese when he first arrived...none of us could! One reason he was popular at school was because his older brother Paul (aged 25) and sister Mella (21), who both lived in England, kept him up to date with all the modern music of the late 90s; M&M, Limp Bizkit, Prodigy etc. He was playing music that hadn't reached the mountains of Portugal yet, and all the local kids were keen to hear it.

His schoolwork was going well except for his English class. He spoke better English than his teacher and she felt threatened by this. One day the teacher was pointing to items in the room and asking different children to name each one. She pointed to the light switch and summoned Craig to say what it was.

"Light switch," answered Craig.

"No, it is a switch light," she insisted. He got rather bored in these basic English lessons so argued the point that 'light switch' was the correct way to say it…he got a detention and an animosity was born between them. Luckily the next year he was able to choose French instead of English on his syllabus.

A couple of years ago, two foals had been born at our farm, now, in their second year, they were hardly foals any more but they were still my babies! Comet was a stocky pony of about 13 hands high; he was a lovely steel grey colour, with a laid-back attitude. His mother Foxy was a sweet little pony from the Spanish mountains; she was a very pretty, liver chestnut colour with a flaxen mane and tail. We had bought her at a horse fair in the north of Portugal. She had been a fantastic mother to Comet, and right from the start, she had allowed me to become his second mum. I had helped him to take his first wobbly steps, and it had been my fingers he had licked to get the first taste of his mother's colostrum. In the first few weeks of his life, he would fall asleep on my lap while I stroked his soft baby coat. It was a wonderful time that I will never forget.

Apollo, Comet's half-brother, was almost black but had white hairs coming through on his face and a line of white hair down the middle of his black ears, which gave away the fact that his coat would not stay black forever, and would eventually become grey. He was bigger than Comet and extremely beautiful, but very nervous. Comet would be easy to train, but Apollo would need a lot of time and patience.

He had inherited his nervous character from his mother who had been born wild in the northern mountains of the Iberian Peninsula and rounded up as a yearling. She had not had good treatment, and was nervous and aggressive when we first bought her. I had spent a lot of time with her, re-assuring her that not all humans were bad, and she had responded well, although she still put her ears back when you first approached her. Steve's nickname for her was Auntie Ears Back, but I called her Tessie.

When Apollo was born, twelve days after Comet, Tessie would not let me get near him; she constantly circled away from me, keeping Apollo on her far side. Hence his first impression of humans was to stay away from them. As he grew, he did come to trust me, and eventually we had a very strong bond.

Tessie was a breed called a Garrano, a small, mountain, hardy pony which in days of old were used to work the land, but as tractors grew in popularity, the breed diminished and Garrano's are now classed as a rare breed. Tessie had given birth to Apollo when she was just two years old, he was a big foal and had taken a lot out of her. Recently I had started riding her, I was a bit big for her but there was no one smaller to start her education. She was about 12.2 hands but very strong, so she wasn't really a child's pony, which was what we needed for the riding holiday business we were trying to start; she was highly strung and very energetic. I knew that she was not really suitable for us but Tessie had already been through a lot in her young life and I was reluctant to think about selling her.

By chance, one day a Dutch couple visited our rented farm where we kept the horses, which was about three kilometres from our house. We started chatting and they introduced themselves as Anki and Berg. They told me that they were interested in rare breeds. They already had rare breeds of sheep and goats on their farm in Holland and at the moment they were looking for the rare Portuguese pony breed called Garranos. They had already bought a stallion and were now looking for two mares. I couldn't believe my ears! Tessie was grazing nearby and their gaze fell on her.

"She is a very nice Garrano" said Anki, "I love her almost black colour and the elongated white star on her forehead...very pretty." They walked slowly and spoke gently to her, I could tell that they were experienced horse people, and they seemed smitten with Tessie. Just as importantly, she seemed to like them. Apollo wandered over to join us and when I told them that he was her son they were amazed. Apollo was now over 14 hands high, he looked every inch a Lusitano; just like his father Silver Moon.

The couple were interested to know about Silver, so I told them the story of how we had rescued him from his stall where he was chained so short that he couldn't even lie down. I told them that he had been gored by a bull in the bullring and was horribly lame and neglected when we had first found him. He was about to be shot, but I begged for his life, and eventually the owner relented and said I could take him. We had brought him home to live out his last years in peace. He had rewarded us with two amazing foals; Comet and Apollo and although we finally had to have him put to sleep, I would never forget him.

The Portuguese are very proud of their Lusitano horse; they are extremely beautiful and very versatile, making wonderful riding horses as well as dressage stars, but they are still used in bullfighting and many horses suffer horrendous injuries.

I told Anki and Berg that Tessie was for sale; I knew this could be a good move for her, to be one of the founders of a new herd of Garranos in Holland. I was sure they would look after her and give her a good life.

CHAPTER 2

CROCODILE CHRISTINE

Leaves had started drifting down from the trees; the long hot summer was slowly coming to an end. The days were still lovely and warm but the nights were cooler. We were still swimming in the river every afternoon, parting with each stroke the fallen floating leaves from the poplar trees that lined the banks. A pair of kingfishers patrolled our stretch of river; they flew just above the water, as fast as bullets, announcing their approach with a long, high-pitched, shrill cry. We always felt privileged to see their bright blue backs overtaking us at incredible speeds as we swam. They nest every year in the river bank, and in June we regularly see the young kingfishers learning to fly and fish. The parents don't help their young, but allow them to stay near their nest for a few days before they chase them away. The young birds don't seem to have fear of us, so we can swim really close to them without them flying away, but within a week of them leaving the nest, the youngsters have all gone in search of their own territories, and the parents are left in peace for another year.

I loved the river which meandered past the bottom of our land; it was the fundamental core that made our home a real paradise. But our swimming days were numbered for this year; when the sun did not shine it was hard to have the will power to brave the chilly water. The nights were drawing in, and soon it would be time to lose another daylight hour. Wood smoke started appearing from our neighbours' chimneys, and ours too, as thoughts turned to the big event of seeing in the new century: New Year 2000.

A large group of us were going to a nightclub for the New Year festivities. Many of our friends were performers at festivals, specialising in juggling, stilt walking in elaborate costumes, mime, fire eating, and dance. They were performing at the nightclub on New Year's Eve, and we had been invited to join them, staying the night in a hotel attached to the nightclub. My daughter Mella was coming to visit from England and bringing her friend Tanya, who was a dancer. Mella attended drama school in London and had done some dancing as part of her studies, so when the booked dancers had to drop out, Mella and Tanya arranged to take their place.

I was pleased for her because she had been having a difficult time in England, and needed to have some fun. Her boyfriend, (whom I am going to call Bruce because he was Australian and I think it is important to change his name for this story), was becoming more and more controlling and autocratic. This clashed with Mella's strong personality, and she wanted to end the relationship, but he had threatened to kill himself if she left him. She was only 21 years old and didn't know how to handle the situation, so she stayed with him, but it couldn't continue. She was staying with us for three weeks, and I hoped that by the time she had to return, she would be strong enough to end her negative relationship with this bully.

An elaborate buffet was laid on for all of the performers, which we happily joined in. Mella was very nervous about dancing on a podium but we all cheered her on and gradually her confidence grew. Craig and his friends were supposed to stay in the hotel, being too young to be at the disco; at first they were happy to do that, they had plenty of food and were having their own party. But as the midnight hour drew closer, they managed to sneak past the doormen, and joined us as we all cheered in the New Year.

The club was only half full; we watched big TV screens showing the New Year in America, Australia, Britain and other countries but it seemed a bit of a damp squid here in Portugal. At about 2 am, just as we were thinking of going to bed, we noticed the club beginning to fill with revellers. When we left next morning to drive home at about 6 am (it had been too noisy to sleep) people were still queuing to get in. I couldn't believe it!

After a foggy drive home, New Year's Day dawned bright and sunny. Steve and I were both a little washed out through lack of sleep and aching all over from so much dancing. I couldn't remember the last time I had been to a discotheque, and I was not in a hurry to repeat the experience, yet I had enjoyed the evening and it was worth the suffering. But what was about to happen next would put a few aches and pains to the back of our minds.

Mella, who had stayed on at the club with Craig, phoned to say that she had danced all night and had just eaten a huge breakfast which the hotel had supplied, and was going to get her head down for a few hours. She told us that Craig had stayed up all night, and was now sound asleep. I went to the horses' farm (which was 3 kilometres from our house) as usual to feed them and muck out their stables with a sore head! Steve decided to go for a motor bike ride to blow away his cobwebs. He arrived home about the same time as me, but he was limping badly and looked battered. He sunk onto the sofa, still in his bike gear, and told me his story.

He had lost control of the bike on a sandy patch of road and the bike had slid under a parked car. He had fallen badly, but jumped to his feet and grabbed the bike, desperate not to be seen lying in the road with his bike stuck under a car. Luckily the parked car was a jeep with high wheels, so neither the bike nor the car were damaged; he kick-started the bike, jumped on and rode home. It was only as he removed his boot that the pain in his leg registered. I could see from his face that he was in a lot of pain, and I could see the leg swelling really fast once it was released from the restrictive boot. His thumb was hanging at a scary angle too and he couldn't move it. I knew we had to get to the hospital fast.

We left the hospital a few hours later after using up all their supplies of plaster of Paris! He had a broken leg and a broken thumb. The young doctor had been great, he had been partying too but still managed to take his shift at A&E and was very helpful and cheerful.

Poor Steve had 6 weeks of bed rest: I knew that it would drive him crazy as there was so much work to be done. Luckily the sun shone for the whole of January, and he would drag himself up onto our veranda every morning, sitting on cushions that I laid on the floor for him. We sat dreaming about what we could do to our house if only we had the finance and a two-legged worker!

A friend took pity on him and gave him an ancient black and white laptop with a floppy disc drive. The laptop had no battery but we had just finished wiring the house for a 12 volt solar system, and it just so happened that our local electrical shop was owned by a genius who loved a challenge. He managed to alter the wiring so that the laptop ran from our 12 volt system. I taught Steve how to type properly instead of with just one finger, and he became quite fast, enjoying typing some funny stories to pass the time

One such story got him into a heap of trouble. He wrote an endearing tale of our dogs Toby and Bica, portraying them as husband and wife. Toby was a handsome strong chap and his wife Bica was a dumb blonde. Bica the dog did have a lovely blonde coat but she wasn't dumb at all, but it made for a funny story. Steve wanted to print his story but we didn't have a printer, so he phoned Hugh, a friend of ours and asked if he would print out his story for him.

We were a bit late arriving at Hugh's house and he was just leaving for a flight to England, so he asked his girlfriend if she would do it for us. We left the floppy disk with her and came home. A few hours later, we had a call from a very irate Hugh who had just landed from his flight to London.

"What did you say to Bica? He shouted down the phone line.

"Who is Bica?" asked Steve innocently.

"My girlfriend," shouted an exasperated Hugh; "her nick name is Bica. She is furious with me and is threatening to throw my computer onto a bonfire because in the story she is characterised as a dumb blonde: she is convinced that I wrote the story. What's it all about?"

Steve had to do a lot of grovelling to Bica, before she finally believed that his story was nothing to do with her and it was just a coincidence that our dog had the same name as her. She hadn't really thrown Hugh's computer onto a bonfire and we did eventually receive the printed story, but sadly it has been lost, which means Steve's masterpiece is trapped inside a floppy disc forever!

Mella was back at college in London but she was not enjoying her drama course as much as she thought she would. She was still with Bruce, and desperately needed to get away. She managed to find a course for young people to go to Israel and live with families there, while teaching the basics of English to children. It could lead to a TEFL certificate (Teaching English as a Foreign Language) which Mella was very keen to have as it would mean she could travel abroad and get a job anywhere...even Portugal. She left her drama college and started on a new adventure; she and a group of other young people set off for Israel.

She would be staying with different Israeli families, teaching their children basic English. It was a fantastic experience for her and she found that she really enjoyed teaching; it seemed she had a flair for connecting with children, and soon the group supervisor gave her a classroom of her own to teach a group of youngsters daily. One thing she learned while staying with Israeli families...never finish all the food on your plate as she had been brought up to do. As soon as her plate was empty it was refilled with delicious food that she couldn't resist, which was not doing her lovely slim outline any good at all!

Whilst in Israel, Mella met an older English woman called Christine who was travelling the world alone. They both shared a love of horses and Christine told her that horses influenced where she travelled to next. Of course Mella mentioned us in Portugal and gave Christine our phone number. A few weeks later Christine phoned me completely out of the blue, asking if we could pick her up from Coimbra railway station. Steve was out at the time but Christine said she didn't mind waiting; it was all part of travelling. He arrived at Coimbra station about two hours later to find it almost deserted.

There was no one waiting who looked in the least bit like a horse rider, so he phoned me to see if I had heard any more from her. While he was on the phone he felt a tap on his shoulder and turning he was confronted by an older woman dressed in a khaki scout uniform, complete with shorts, necktie and toggle!

"Are you Steve" she enquired.

"Yes, you must be Christine, I like your hat". She was wearing an Australian bushman's hat. She and Steve chatted all the way home; Steve had lived in Australia for 13 years and loved the chance to reminisce. Christine had lived with a cowhand in the Australian bush for two years and was full of stories of her tough hard life there. They were already firm buddies by the time they arrived back at our farm.

We called her Crocodile Christine as she had more adventure stories to tell than the great man himself! She told us that she was exhausted and needed to stay somewhere quiet for a while to

15

recoup her energy. By now we had turned one of our downstairs dirt floored rooms into a lovely bedroom with its own bathroom. We had concreted the dirt floor and laid oak floorboards, the walls were all whitewashed with lime, and it looked really cosy. We had our first horse riding booking of the year coming shortly and they would be staying in the new bedroom, which meant our caravan, that had previously been our guest accommodation, was free.

Christine was thrilled; it was just what she needed. Some of the stories she told us about how she had shared accommodation in Turkey and India, with just a dirty sheet between beds for privacy, and drunken fights breaking out in the middle of the night, sounded like the plot of a horror film! She told us that she would be 60 in a few weeks...what a gutsy lady. She was on a tight budget so we made an arrangement that she could stay for as long as she liked and maybe ride once or twice a week. In return she would help me muck out and look after the horses.

It worked out really well, she was good fun to ride with, and told me that she had six grown up children in England whom she hadn't seen or been in contact with for a long time. I detected a note of sadness in her voice as she talked of her family, but she changed the subject which I took to mean that she didn't want to talk about that part of her life.

It was soon time for our first guests of the year to arrive. Penny and John; were a very nice, slightly reserved couple. Penny was a good rider who took part in dressage competitions, John was a mountain biker, who had brought his own bike with him on the plane from England; our local area is fantastic for hard core mountain biking, with its steep tricky downhill tracks, as well as mountain peaks to climb. He and Steve pored over ordnance survey maps to plot out some routes for him to ride throughout the week while Penny, Christine and I were horse riding. I was a little worried about how the two ladies would get along. Penny was quiet and reserved whilst Christine was a rather loud extrovert, and had a habit of singing rugby songs whilst riding, which I found hilarious. I needn't have worried, it wasn't long before Penny was learning the words and all three of us were singing bawdy rugby songs and scaring away the wildlife whilst trotting through the mountains.

Christine's 60th birthday fell midweek during Penny and John's holiday with us. I planned to cook a good old Aussie bush meal of bangers and beans over a fire in our yard. We invited some friends of ours called Mark and Trish who were also great travellers, and as a birthday present to Christine, I offered her the use of our telephone to speak to her family in England.

It was expensive to make international calls, and I assumed that was the reason she hadn't been in contact with her family. She seemed a bit reluctant and I wondered if I had done the right thing, but eventually she made a call. I heard her son's reaction from across the room.

"Mum...I can't believe it's you. We have been so worried". She had tears in her eyes and a huge smile on her face, so I left the room and went back to my friends and guests. Her son gave our number to his siblings so that they could all be in contact with their mother again. I don't know why the family silence had started, but I hoped that it had been broken now. Meanwhile Penny, my quiet retiring guest, and my friend Trish, were giggling uncontrollably and rather a little drunk! When Christine came back outside to sit around the fire, she started up her rugby songs and the evening wore on into the night. She later told us that she was returning to England, but not for long, and she was already planning her next adventure.

A couple of years later, Mark and Trish met up with Christine whilst hiking on the Inca trail in Peru. Still travelling...I wonder if we will ever get another phone call completely out of the blue; I wouldn't be surprised.

Adam, the young guy who had sold us our house, had bought another renovation project not far from us. Things hadn't worked out with his girlfriend in Scotland and he had come back to Portugal to live. One day he was driving along the road into Góis when he picked up three men hitchhiking. They were Belarusian and had been working for a Portuguese company that had gone bust. Because they were staying here illegally, the company didn't pay them for the month's work that they had done, and the men could do nothing about it. They had no money and nowhere to stay.

Adam offered them accommodation, food, and a wage, in exchange for help with building work. They readily jumped at the chance and turned out to be skilled builders, ready to work hard—as long as you kept the vodka locked away! Other foreigners were queuing up to employ them, including us. When our turn came, they moved into the caravan and were a huge help to us in building up our newly acquired ruin.

The oldest man was called Ivan; he was fearsome looking with a mouth full of gold teeth and cropped grey hair; he was built like a wrestler and was probably around 40 years old. He told us in broken English and a smattering of Portuguese that he had left his wife and two children behind in Belarus. He was trying to earn money to pay for his children's education and to give them all a better standard of living. He missed them dreadfully and had no idea when he would be able to return. Ivan showed me a couple of crumpled photos of his family, I felt so sorry for him.

The other two Belarusians, Maxim and Mikhail were much younger, probably only in their early twenties. Maxim had a girlfriend living in Belarus; she was always phoning him on his old mobile phone. We had no signal at our house, so whenever his phone rang, he sprinted up to the top of our nearest hill where he could get a weak phone signal. He was planning to leave Portugal and go to Paris where he had friends working for much better money. They told us that it was dangerous to travel as they were illegal immigrants. I must admit, I thought they were exaggerating a little.

Ivan and Mikhail worked hard; they didn't want any time off, and were happy to work seven days a week. We got used to their laughter and singing from the rooftop as they worked, the vodka bottles mounting up in our recycling! A few weeks after Maxim had left for Paris, Mikhail had some terrible news: his friend had been killed. Mikhail couldn't find out any details and just seemed to resign himself to the fact that there was nothing he could do, but a great sadness fell over the pair; and us too. It seemed that they had not been exaggerating after all.

One evening, a few weeks later, we heard a dog barking constantly; the poor dog carried on barking all through the night. The next morning Steve and I decided to try to find out where the barking was coming from. It seemed to be coming from the forest on the other side of the river. Sadly, it was still common practise to set traps for wild boar. Only the year before, we had rescued a small dog trapped in a snare. It was badly injured and very aggressive, so

Steve had come home and put on his thick motor bike jacket and gloves and using a pair of wire cutters, he had managed to free the poor creature, which fled, with the noose still tightly secured around its torso. We desperately hoped that the little dog returned to its home and the owners were able to break the noose.

The bark that we were now hearing was from a much bigger dog. We drove to a bridge and parked up on the other side of the river. He must have heard us talking and tramping through the forest because the barking stopped. How could we find him now? We searched and searched for an hour or more but the dog didn't start barking again; eventually we gave up and returned home. Later that afternoon, the barking started again. I knew I couldn't leave the dog another night trapped and probably injured in the forest, so I drove back and searched again, keeping as quiet as I could. There was still no sign of him. Then I heard a whining sound coming from the river; I ran down to the river bank, and there standing up to his belly in fast running water was a poor very bedraggled dog.

He was trapped by a long rope that was tied around his neck and had become entangled in rocks and branches underwater. He must have been trying to cross the river, dragging his rope behind him; probably on the scent of a female dog. He was overjoyed to see me, but how was I going to reach him? There was only one thing for it; I took off my socks, shoes and trousers, and scrambled across the slippery rocks until I was close to him, then, crouching down, I talked gently to him.

He seemed friendly enough, so I inched forward and delved my arms under the cold water to try to find out how he was trapped. I could feel a solid tree branch that had probably floated down the river and got caught up in this rocky section of water. The rope was frayed and had snagged firmly on the branch, but as I pulled it in the opposite direction, it came away quite easily and the dog was free. I just managed to stumble back across the rocks and grab the end of the rope before the dog took off.

He was very unsteady on his feet, he must have been freezing; his coat was thick, and had probably saved his life. He looked like a Serra da Estrela mountain dog, probably not a pure bred, but he had the rather scary amber eyes of that breed. He seemed friendly, so I decided the best thing would be to take him home and give him a good meal, then start looking for his owners. Over the next few days we contacted the police and local vets, we put up a notice in the local supermarket, but nobody claimed him. Our Belarusian workers adopted him and took him into their caravan, they called him Big Dog. This worked well for us because our two dogs, Toby and Bica, and our three cats, BB, Robin and Misty, were not at all happy to have this huge wolf sharing their home. We really needed to find his owner.

We had another unexpected tiny addition to our family; a little half poodle puppy that we had named Moppy. A week earlier, we had taken our workers to the market town of Arganil. We had stayed in Arganil for a month when we first arrived in Portugal, so knew the town well. The hot and spicy barbecued chicken that was served at the market was a real treat, and we were all looking forward to it. I wandered from one market stall to another, not really planning on buying much, when my gaze fell on a large basket full of tiny fluffy black puppies.

It was not uncommon for people to try to give away or sell puppies at the market, and they were so cute that I just had to stop and stroke them. Just at that moment, some children ran up and started picking up the puppies and running around with them. An old woman wrapped in a shawl and brandishing a stick hobbled over to the children and shouted at them to put the puppies down.

"Will you take one?" she begged me, "My husband says if I come home with them, he is leaving me, I have so many there is no room for him in the bed." The old woman went on to explain to me that she bred poodles, but the mother of these babies had been a bad girl and run off with a street dog, she didn't have a clue what breed the father was or what he looked like.

The mother of two of the children, who had been terrorising the puppies, waddled over; she had a stall at the market selling second hand clothes. She was very rotund; her fat wrists were jangling with bangles and her greasy hair was scraped back into an untidy bun. Her sandaled feet were filthy and she looked rather grumpy, but when she saw the puppies, her face broke into a big smile. The children had obviously been asking their mother if they could have one of the puppies.

"Yes, they are cute, you can have one each" she bawled with a dismissive flip of her hand, before she waddled back to her market stall. The children grabbed two of the poor little pups and ran off after their mother. The old woman looked crestfallen but just shrugged. Then, turning to me, she again begged me to take one. I shook my head and turned to leave, I knew Steve would kill me if I took on any more animals, we already had two dogs, three cats, numerous ducks and chickens and seven horses.

We were drawn by our noses to the barbeque area and sat at an old trestle table on small wobbly stools under the shade of huge mulberry trees, which were dropping their fruits underfoot. The smells of food being barbecued in the smoky air was irresistible, and the Portuguese diners were all in high spirits, there was much shouting and laughing and copious amounts of rough red wine being consumed. For a lot of Portuguese people, especially the older folk from the mountain villages, these weekly markets were essential, not only for buying and selling produce, but as a social event where gossip was shared.

Our Belarusian friends enjoyed the atmosphere and seemed happier than I had seen them since the death of their friend. As we were finishing our food, I felt a tap on my shoulder, and looking around I came face to face with the old woman with the pups. In her arms she had a tiny little scrap of black curly fur which she placed in my lap.

"Please take her," she croaked, "she's the smallest one." The little pup crawled up from my lap and snuggled into my neck, making the cutest little mewling noises. She was so soft, I didn't want to give her back but Steve was glaring at me! I lifted her up; she had the most adorable face and little black eyes. She was so helpless; on impulse I handed her to Steve and before he could refuse, she crawled up into his neck. I could hear the little noises she was making, and I saw the look of a smitten man cross his face.

She came home with us, and after hungrily eating some moistened cat biscuits and little bits of chicken, I took her into Craig's bedroom which was still the quietest, safest room in the house, and stroked her until she fell asleep on his bed. When Craig came home from school, he couldn't believe his eyes; he named her Moppy, which was a great name because she looked just like a mini mop. Our Belarusian friends called her Švabra which was Mop in their language!

CHAPTER 3

FARMYARD FROLICKS

Big Dog was causing problems, he chased our ducks and chickens, and after he almost caught one, we decided to keep them in their pen, which they were very indignant about. They were used to having the run of the farm during the daytime, and they strutted up and down along the fence line of their pen squabbling with each other and pecking at the mesh. Our farmyard fences were no match for Big Dog either, and he was soon jumping out and running off. I knew that a dog of his size with a taste for chickens would not be tolerated by our neighbours.

He also bullied our dogs. Toby was 12 years old and had always been 'top dog' and Bica was a lovely kind girl who had mothered Moppy right from day one. It was horrible to see them afraid to go out into their own yard; he was such a huge lumbering affectionate beast, (to humans) that I couldn't help but like him, but I was aware that he could squash little tiny Mop with one huge playful bear-like paw. I had no choice but to put him on a chain. He seemed used to it and didn't complain; he had been dragging a long, frayed rope when I had found him in the river so I was pretty sure that he had been kept in this way before.

One day Steve went to our local builder's yard to buy building materials. He was friendly with Antonio the foreman and remembered that when he had last visited about a year ago, there had been a young dog there, not much more than a puppy. He asked Antonio what had happened to his dog and he told Steve that it had got loose and run away a few weeks ago. He seemed genuinely sad. The wheels started to turn in Steve's brain....

"I think it may be your dog that we have at our farm, would you like to come and see?" A big grin lit up Antonio's kind, ruddy face and he said he would come to see if the dog was his in his lunch break. Big Dog heard Antonio's truck arriving and recognised the sound of the engine. He was leaping and barking in excitement as Antonio walked into our yard whistling to his dog; they obviously had a strong connection. Big Dog jumped up and put his paws on the man's shoulders, he really was more like a bear than a dog! They left together, with the dog sitting up front in the truck, his lovely big head hanging out of the window, and tranquillity returned to our little piece of Paradise.

The tranquillity didn't last for long. One Saturday afternoon, little Moppy became ill. Her small body was convulsing and she was having trouble breathing. I looked inside her mouth and her tongue was swollen up. I thought she was going to die. She looked as if she had been poisoned, but how was that possible? She had not been outside of our farmyard. Veterinary practices were not common at this time in the mountains of Portugal; we had used a vet in Arganil a few years ago, and he was useless. We had heard of a vet in Coimbra but that was an hour's drive away. I was not sure little Mop would make it, but we phoned anyway. The practise was just closing, but they said they would wait for us to get there. She lay still in my arms on the journey, and was struggling to breathe. The vet seemed as flummoxed as we were. However, she had a young trainee vet working with her, who introduced herself as Nicolette. She had been listening to our conversation, and came over to ask her superior if she could examine Moppy.

"Do you live near a pine forest?" asked Nicolette

"Yes, we do." I answered, desperate for somebody to help us.

"I think your little puppy has digested, or maybe played with a processionary pine caterpillar. I was brought up in the countryside and have seen these symptoms before. Children and even adults can be affected by their poisonous hairs."

"Can you cure her?" I asked with tears welling up in my eyes.

"We can try. The poison is in her tongue; I will give her a local anaesthetic and try to remove the poisonous microscopic hairs.

The poison is travelling up into her eye. Can you see it is turning white? She may be blind in that eye."

"Oh no, that's awful, poor little girl." I stroked her tiny head as Nicolette continued.

"The poison has already damaged her tongue; it will depend on how much of her tongue remains. In a few days' time we will know. Dogs need their tongues, not only to eat and drink, but to pant," she explained.

"I will give her an antihistamine, and you can take her home. Keep her cool and use cold water on her tongue to take down the swelling." Nicolette gave me some high protein paste to feed her by smoothing it over her tongue, and told me to keep her tongue as damp as possible. She gave me a portable drip to keep her hydrated.

Poor little Mop's tongue turned grey and about one third of it fell away, but she survived. Her eyesight was not affected, but she always ate and drank messily with her two thirds of a tongue!

Nicolette opened up her own practice a few years later, and I was one of her first clients and still am today.

Our Muscovy ducks had been given to us as tiny chicks by our neighbour Francisco. As chicks they had been yellow and brown but as they matured they had beautiful white and black feathers, with red around the head. We had three ducks and one drake. They used to fly down to the river every morning but always returned after an hour or two.

They laid large white eggs which tasted delicious. They each laid one egg a day for approximately 12 days then, they would stop and get broody, wanting to sit on their eggs. We would take nine eggs from each duck for ourselves, but always left three eggs for each of them to sit on and hatch out new little ducklings. The three female adult ducks were called Puddleduck, Wiggles and Lucky Ducky. They were very sweet and loved me to stroke their backs and tickle them under the chin. The drake was huge and not very friendly; his name was Moby Duck.

We had three lovely brown chickens that would come to call. If I had a treat for them, I would call out "Where's my girls?" in a high-pitched voice, and they would come running. They loved to sit on my lap, which could be vexing if we were eating al fresco because they would steal food from my plate!

A neighbour of mine had a small farm but sadly she had to give it up for health reasons. She managed to give away all of her chickens but could not find a home for her cockerel. Like a fool I offered to take him, and I very soon regretted my decision, as from the moment he arrived he dominated the whole farm.

He hated me, because my chickens, which were now his of course, came running to me when I called them. This infuriated him and he would chase me doggedly around the farm. It got to the point that I was scared to come out of the house! I would creep down the steps and hear the patter patter of his feet running across the yard. He was a big bird with nasty talons; he would leap up in the air and throwing his legs forward, attack me with those talons. I would try to dodge him around the car, but when I looked underneath to see which way he was heading, all I saw was his beady eye, watching me! He would then come hurtling around, startling me with his amazing velocity.

I had found a large thick piece of cardboard in our shed and used it as a shield: but still he attacked. Steve would just laugh, thinking I was exaggerating, but one day for no reason, the evil beast flew at Steve, tearing a lump from his leg. His instinct was to defend himself; he picked up his old crutch which was still propped up against a shed from when he had broken his leg. The killer cockerel came around for a second attack and Steve's crutch connected with its head; the cockerel looked dazed and fell to the ground. Steve quickly killed him, and thinking I would be pleased, he held the dead cockerel up for me to see. Craig and I both burst into tears! But when we recovered from the shock, we all enjoyed the best coq au vin I had ever tasted!

Steve was very keen on self-sufficiency; he already had a big veggie garden and had planted some fruit trees. We had inherited two amazing old olive trees which we had harvested regularly. A normal harvest was about 85 kilos of olives which we took to our local olive mill. The mill cold pressed our olives and gave us 1 litre of extra virgin oil for every 10 kilos of olives. The pungent peppery taste was wonderful as a salad dressing. The mill then kept our olives and re-pressed them with everyone else's in the area to sell commercially.

Olives are such wonderful trees; we think our two are more than 250 years old. Blue tits nest in them every year, as do long-tailed tits, making use of the mossy bark to line their nests. Around the base of the trees, there were plenty of crevices and holes where insects of all descriptions found homes, and on wet nights it was the best place to find toads and salamanders emerging into the night. We rolled two large rocks underneath the boughs, and would often sit there with a beer on warm nights, enjoying the tree's peaceful aura.

News had spread about our killer cockerel, and one day our neighbour Francisco passed by and offered us a replacement. Francisco was a short squat man of around 55 years of age; he had a lovely kind face and beautiful liquid brown eyes. He was never without his flat cap, and he loved to tell yarns.

We walked the 300 metres to his house with him, he was our favourite neighbour, full of advice and surprises. Steve got on very well with him, he had taught us so much about Portuguese country living. We now knew how to look after our olive, orange, lemon, quince, persimmon and pomegranate trees, and which diseases our grapevines suffered from, and how to treat them organically. He had a moon chart; lots of people did in this area, in fact you could buy one in the local agricultural shop, and still can today. He would consult his chart and tell us when to grow particular vegetables. He even brought me along some lettuce seedlings, and described in detail how to serve lettuce!

"Firstly, you wash the leaves, pat them dry and add salt."

"Enjoy," he added, kissing the air with his thumb and forefinger. He really thought us northern city people didn't know how to prepare lettuce! And nowadays when lettuce is pre-washed in chlorine and packed in gas filled bags...maybe he was right.

Francisco dexterously picked out a beautiful young cockerel from his chicken pen and handed him to us. He was a real beauty, black and white speckled with a healthy looking red comb. He wouldn't take any payment, but asked us if he could take the branches we had pruned from our olive trees, for his goats to nibble; we thought that was a great swap! We called our new cockerel Chico, which is the nickname often used for anyone called Francisco.

Chico matured into a very nice friendly cockerel, I was very fond of him; whenever he found an insect or worm, or I left out some titbits, he always called his girls Fanny, Franny, and Freaky to take first pick. He stood back while they pecked at the tastiest titbits; he was a true gentleman. Unfortunately our male duck Moby became more and more aggressive towards Chico as he matured. Chico tried to stay away from him but Moby started chasing him relentlessly.

One day I was relaxing on our veranda when I heard Chico cry in alarm. I looked over the rails and to my horror, saw him being chased by Moby down the garden path towards the river. I heard a splash as Chico ran straight off a terraced wall into the water. I ran down as fast as I could, Moby was standing on top of the wall aggressively pacing up and down but when I flapped my arms at him, he waddled back up the hill. I lay down on the terrace wall and just managed to reach the poor drowned Chico.

I hugged him to me but his neck just lolled down and his eyes were closed. I tried to rub his body but got no response so I thought the best thing would be to leave him in his roosting shed in the dark. I made sure he was lying in plenty of straw and closed the door. I really thought that we had lost him but about half an hour later I heard a weak familiar call… "Cock-a-doodle doo." I opened his door, and with a ruffle of his feathers he was out of the door and calling to his harem as if nothing had happened. But something had happened; and I had to make a choice of which one was staying and which one was leaving.

It often happens that as one door closes another opens, and that is what happened for Moby Drake. Our friend Adam came for dinner that evening and of course I recited the adventures of the day.

"I will take him" he proffered with a grin. "I love duck." Adam was looking to shock me and he succeeded. Luckily he was only joking; he explained that he was jealous of our duck eggs (which we didn't share with anyone!) and had been thinking of keeping ducks himself. He promised he would go to the market the next day, buy a couple of female ducks and pick Moby up on the way home. It was a win-win situation. Two ducks from the market would have a good home instead of being eaten, Moby would have a new family and Adam would have his own supply of duck eggs and not have to pester us for ours!

We had eight young ducklings already running around the farm as well as the three mother ducks and had begun to realise that ducks were really messy. Steve was going to cull the youngsters once they were full grown so I didn't name them or bond with them in any way. I was learning to be self-sufficient; they would have a short but wonderful life here on the farm, and then they would meet their demise. We had already hatched a plan for their death.

Steve had built a concrete home for all the ducks and chickens to share, when Francisco saw it, his eyes opened wide.

"It's a hotel!" he exclaimed. It was very grand and the fowl all seemed very content to live in there at night and run free all day. In the mornings, when I opened the hotel door, they all rushed out, almost falling over each other in their excitement to be out in the sunshine. Our plan was for me to catch one of the young ducks as they came out of the door, and Steve would pin it to the ground and chop off its head. It might sound barbaric, but the whole procedure would only take a few seconds. Already some of the male ducklings were starting to annoy the females, jumping onto their backs and biting their necks. It became obvious which ones were next for the chop!

We didn't have enough electricity from our solar to run a freezer, so we could only kill one at a time. We would have enough meat to last us through the winter. Our three female ducks, Puddleduck, Wiggles and Lucky Ducky seemed very content without Moby continually pestering them and they still laid clutches of eggs which were delicious. One day Steve had the idea to put some fertilised chicken eggs under Puddleduck who was the broodiest of the three ducks. Our chickens didn't seem to be very good at sitting on eggs; I think they had been bred as egg layers and they'd had the broodiness bred out of them; they showed no interest in procreating.

Puddleduck successfully hatched out three baby chickens. We were delighted, and so was she. The next few weeks were a learning curve for us all, including Puddleduck who loved her little chicks. Muscovy ducks do not quack; they are silent, whereas a mother chicken is constantly calling her chicks to her. Our little chicks would wander off but then not be able to find their mother; it was a full-time job to keep reuniting them, but that was only the beginning. When they were a few weeks old, Puddleduck decided it was time to take her babies for a swim.

Our water supply was a natural spring on our land. We planned to dig a bore hole, but at that moment we were still using our spring water. We caught it in bottles and buckets as it cascaded down from the mountain during the winter, but as summer advanced the spring water dropped to a trickle, giving us just enough water for drinking.

The water we didn't catch made a small pond which was full of frogs and tadpoles in springtime. Puddleduck led her babies down to the pond and tried her utmost to encourage them to swim, but those little chicks would not even get their feet wet. They ran up and down chirruping, but they would not enter the water: poor Puddleduck was very confused. Apart from the fact that the chicks would never be accompanying the ducks when they flew down to the river for a swim, the chicks grew happy and healthy. The other thing was...they always drank like a duck! They would fill their little beaks with water and hold their heads back to swallow just like their mother duck; it was very funny to watch.

Francisco was leaning on our gatepost one morning, in the middle of yet another yarn about a genet he had caught in his chicken pen, and on which he was now in the process of practicing his taxidermy skills, when our three half grown chickens came running across the yard.

"Ah, I see you have three young cockerels there" he said with a furrowing of his brow and a knowing nod. We had been wondering what sex they were, everyone told us it was very hard to tell until they were older, but we had hoped for at least one female to add to Chico's harem. After another couple of weeks we knew that he had been right...of course!

The young cocks started fighting and trying to mount the females, poor Fanny, Franny and Freaky had blood on their necks where the youngsters constantly tried to mate with them. Chico tried his best to defend them, but he was outnumbered.

What we needed was a freezer, but we still didn't have electricity to the house, only the small solar system which would not even support a fridge. We had heard that the electricity company was offering grants to people living in old houses like ours, and we were tempted to apply. Our nearest electricity was 300 metres away so we would need about six posts along the road, plus all the wiring etc. We loved the idea of solar power, but to have a system big enough for all our growing needs would cost more money than we could afford. The quote we received from the electricity company was reasonable. We decided to go for it.

CHAPTER 4

HENRIQUE THE HORRID

What an exciting day it was when our electricity was finally connected. The light bulbs and switches had already been in place for a month, The concrete posts had been erected all along the road, just waiting for the technicians to arrive and connect up all of the wiring. When their work was done, we ran around from room to room, like excited children, switching on all of the lights. I'm sure the technicians thought we were bonkers but they laughed along with us as they cleared away their tools.

Our house, which had only ever been lit by candles, oil lamps and our very poor solar system, was lit up like a Christmas tree. The spiders danced uneasily on their labyrinth of gossamer webs, before unseen. Craig had been saving all of his birthday and Christmas money for years and now he couldn't wait to go shopping.

We all planned a day trip into Coimbra which was our nearest city. We had the dilemma of choosing lamp shades for an ancient house that had never had lighting before. Modern bright lighting might look bizarre so we were looking for old fashioned lamps, based on a candle design. We found some lovely wall lamps that looked like old fashioned oil lanterns, they were expensive but we thought they would look appropriate. Craig eagerly anticipated visiting the big electrical stores in search of a TV, a music system, and a play station. We arrived home with a car boot full of parcels!

Some time afterwards, my father died. He was 78, but had been ill since he was 49 years old. As a lad in 1942, he had enlisted into the air force at Calshot, near Portsmouth, and had learnt how to maintain the sea planes that flew from the base. He also worked with the air force in Greece. I have some lovely old black and white photos of my handsome young father, proudly standing next to a sea plane that he was working on, his blonde curls fighting against copious amounts of Brylcreem! He always told stories about how exciting the time was for him: a young 16-year-old boy from a very sheltered upbringing, suddenly finding himself in the middle of a huge adventure.

After the war, he went to work with his father in their hardware shop. In those days, asbestos was widely used in the building industry, and he spent many hours cutting asbestos into different sized strips to sell over the counter. His father became ill at a young age, but of course nobody linked his illness to asbestos poisoning. I can remember visiting my grandparents in Bognor Regis as a child, and my granddad would be lying on a bed that was made up for him in the lounge room. I was always a little bit afraid of him, and used to hide behind my mother when he beckoned me to sit with him.

Later in my dad's life, he went into hospital for an operation on a hiatus hernia. Sadly, the operation agitated the asbestos that was lying dormant in his lungs. He had long ugly scars left from an operation to try to remove the asbestos, but it wasn't successful, and left him with a lot of pain from the surgery. He couldn't work anymore as his breathing was so bad, so he took a voluntary job as a driver for W.R.V.S. (Women's Royal Voluntary Service) delivering free meals to old or infirm people in their own homes. He lived for another thirty years, always dogged by pain, but he never lost his sense of humour, and always had a smile on his face, and his old pipe smouldering in his hand.

Craig and I went back to England for his funeral, leaving Steve to manage everything on the farm. It was a very sad time for all of the family, but it was good to catch up with Paul, my eldest son, who told me he was coming to visit in the summer, and would be bringing his new girlfriend to meet us. Mella flew back from Israel, her granddad had looked after her a lot when she was young, and she had loved him dearly. It was lovely to see my mother, brother and sister and their ever-growing families for the first time in over a year. My parents were divorced, but had stayed good friends, my dad was still a big part of my mum's life, and she would miss him more than any of us. Many tears were shed, but also many hugs shared, and lots of laughter as we all reminisced on our upbringing with our wonderful father. He was a much-loved husband, father of three, and grandfather of six, and he left me an inheritance that would enable us to install water at our home.

We had a quote from a bore hole specialist company; they would drill the hole, which ended up being 120 metres deep, and install a pump and all the plumbing to bring water into taps; not only to the house, but all around the farm. The mess created by a 120 metre hole was unbelievable, the company cleared up most of the rubble that had been dug up, but the whole area was covered in thick grey sludge that they had to drill through before reaching good pure water. Mother Nature worked her rejuvenating magic, and within a year, the area was green again. Hoses were bought to water the gardens. No more lugging heavy buckets of water for us; oh, what luxury...Thanks Dad!

Our horses still lived at a rented farm which was three kilometres from our house. They had lived there for seven years and had been happy and content overall, but all was about to change. One morning when I went as usual to feed them, there was a stranger waiting for me, holding on to two unknown horses. He wore his hair brushed back from his lofty brow, and large glasses sat on his rather bulbous nose. He had an arrogant air about him that raised the hairs on the back of my neck, as he told me that he had permission from the president of Góis, who was a friend of his, to keep his horses at the farm.

I couldn't see how this was possible, there were only three stables and I had 6 horses living there. Guv and Smartie were old and great friends so they shared a large barn together. Roxy was a Welsh Cob and found Portuguese weather easy to cope with, so he lived outside with just a shelter. Comet and Apollo shared the second stable and the third small stable was for Foxy. The horses were turned out on ten acres during the day, and only stabled at night.

Although the man, who introduced himself as Henrique, had seemed polite enough at first, his horses were very scruffy and thin and I didn't like the rough way he handled them. His mare was pregnant but he didn't seem to care, and lifted his boot to kick her when she tried to pull away from him. Both horses were wary of him, showing the whites of their eyes, and pulling back from him as he gesticulated with his free hand. He was telling, not asking me, where he should stable his horses. He didn't ask me if I would be willing to share the barn with him: he told me.

I had to admit that the barn which Guv and Smartie shared was just about big enough to make four small stables, which was his plan. He was willing to get builders in to do the work, but it was his attitude that really bothered me.

Another problem was that he wanted to keep his horses staked out on long ropes during the daytime. This wouldn't work with my horses running free as they could get tangled up in the ropes. Also, one of his horses was a stallion and I had five geldings and a mare. I didn't want any more foals but I knew what a little flirt Foxy was!

The gelding of horses and castration of dogs were not common at that time in the mountains. Lots of horses were stallions, and when I told Henrique that all my horses had been castrated, he literally crossed his legs in horror!

Our very good friends, Trish and Mark, had bought a small farm way off the beaten track; they only had a small motorbike for transport, but needed some manure for their land as they wanted to be self-sufficient and grow lots of veggies. Trish came up with the idea of us lending them Foxy for a month or two, to graze their land and help them out with their manure shortage. They were also buying a couple of goats so she would have some company, and it would give me time to consider what I wanted to do about the situation with Henrique and his stallion. It seemed like a good idea, so a few days later I set off to ride Foxy over the mountains to her new temporary home.

I had studied the area on our large scale maps and had worked out a route which would take me into new territory that I had not explored before. I really enjoyed the challenge of finding new routes, and as Foxy and I rode higher and the wind picked up, the tracks had a very different feel to them. Sometimes I rode, and sometimes I walked beside her, stroking her ears, and just enjoying the moment. We passed through a rather bleak old north facing village, where it seemed the sun never reached. The houses were all built of slate from the surrounding hillside, half of the houses were derelict, and I felt a damp chill creeping into my bones. It was a different world from our lush green sheltered valley down by the river, but as I rode around to the eastern side of the mountain, and started the long descent into Mark and Trish's valley, the sun was there waiting to warm me once again.

As I rounded a corner, a startled herd of deer gracefully galloped up the rock-strewn track ahead of us, their white tails standing up in alarm as they swerved from the track and blended into the thick heather and gorse bushes. Ahead of me was a forest of beautiful chestnut trees; they had probably grown there because of an underground water course. Foxy crunched underfoot the fallen fruits, mostly still encased in their green spiky shells. Chestnuts were a staple food for mountain folk in bygone days, and are still collected and enjoyed today as tasty treats.

After spending two months with Mark and Trish, it was time for Foxy to return. The weather was turning cold and wet and she had eaten all of the grass. Steve dropped me up at their farm on his off-road motor bike, and I rode her to her new home. I had already made the decision about her future.

There was a family in Góis who had a stallion, he was a real beauty; I had met the young owner a few times while out riding. On one occasion before she went on holiday to Trish's farm, Foxy was with us on a ride. She was being ridden by a young girl with lots of experience luckily…because as the young man came past us on his stallion, it whinnied to Foxy, and she wanted to leave us and follow it. The girl managed to turn Foxy back towards us, but the two horses whinnied to each other until they were out of earshot.

Later that afternoon, the young owner had visited me to ask if I would sell Foxy as his horse needed a companion, and he would like to breed a foal, also his sister wanted her own horse so that they could ride together. I had said that she was not for sale at the time, but because of the circumstances, I realised that I had made the wrong decision. I didn't see how I could cope with flirty Foxy and Henrique's stallion living at the farm together safely, so sadly I made the hard decision to sell her. I rode her straight to her new home, and could almost see Foxy blushing and batting her lashes at the handsome stallion. It seemed that I had made the right choice for her, she settled in to her new home well, and the following spring, we learned that she was in foal.

After his initial attempts at being congenial, Henrique's manner changed towards me. He liked to intimidate and criticise the way that I looked after my horses. He declared that he didn't understand my Portuguese, which I would agree was not perfect, but others seemed to understand me. He actually spoke good English but refused to speak it with me. He was a professor and very well thought of; the local people called him Sir, which I'm sure he loved, but he didn't fool me, he had a very nasty side to him, and he was cruel to his horses.

If I was giving a lesson in our school, he would criticise my teaching methods, saying it was not the correct Portuguese way and that the pupils should allow him to teach them. Some did, but most came back to me saying that he shouted at them, and his horses were too nervous and fidgety.

I started to leave my horses out in the field at night while his two were stabled, and bring my horses into the stables in the daytime when his were staked out on their ropes, this seemed to work quite well for a while but it wasn't to last.

We were expecting a couple to come for a week's riding holiday. When they arrived they were keen to meet the horses that they would be riding, so I drove them to the stables to meet Guv and Smartie; I would be riding Roxy as usual. I had been working all three horses daily, and although they still had some of their winter coats, I had groomed them until they gleamed. Stuart and Gill were a nice young couple who took part in 3-day-event competitions in England. They were looking forward to some fast rides, so the horses had been getting extra oats!

Early in the mornings, when the guests were enjoying their breakfast at our house, I would leave on my little scooter to travel to the horse farm. Once there, I would bring the horses into the stables and feed them their breakfast. Once Stuart and Gill had finished their breakfast, and were ready for their day of riding, Steve drove them the three kilometres to the stables.

The weather was great and we had some wonderful rides, but on the last day of their holiday, I arrived as usual to feed the horses in the morning, and was horror struck to see Henrique's stallion running loose in the field with my geldings. Even from afar, I could see blood on Guv's back, and blood trickling down Smartie's white neck. My little 'pit bull' cob, Roxy, was chasing the stallion, who was much bigger than him. Roxy turned and kicked hard with both back feet, he connected with the stallion's shoulder; the horse seemed to quieten and limp back towards the safety of his stable. I ran to shut the stable door, I felt really bad, and could already see the horse's shoulder beginning to swell, but I had to catch my horses and assess their injuries.

Guv's injuries were the worst; he had a bite on his back with torn skin hanging down, Smartie seemed a bit lame and had minor cuts, Roxy, Comet and Apollo all seemed unscathed. Just at that moment, Steve arrived with Stuart and Gill, both looking forward to their last picnic day ride.

Their mouths opened in shock at the sight before them. Henrique arrived just after, and as I told him what had happened, he threw some hay into his horse's stable and stormed off without a word.

We knew of a Dutch couple who lived about half an hour away in Arganil, they were running a similar business to ours, offering horse rides into the mountains. Steve contacted them and asked if they would be able to take our guests out for a day ride at such short notice. They were happy to help, so while I patched up poor Guv and Smartie, Steve took Stuart and Gill over to Arganil to enjoy their last day on someone else's horses.

When Henrique returned, he was very angry that his horse was lame as he had planned a big ride out with his friends from Coimbra. The farrier was due to shoe his horse that morning, and when he arrived, Henrique ordered the farrier to tie the horse up to a concrete post, with his head only a few inches from the ground so that the poor horse, who had a very bruised shoulder, could not protest at being made to stand on three legs: then he left.

It was awful to watch; the animal was obviously in pain and should be rested for a week or so. I tried to reason with the farrier, but he said he needed the work, and couldn't risk upsetting Henrique, who had told him that he was starting a riding school at the farm, and was already in the process of buying more horses. I had been told nothing of this plan and arrived back home feeling very demoralized.

Next evening, when I arrived to feed my horses and turn them out for the night, there was a new horse stumped out on a rope, a stunning palomino stallion. He was galloping round and around, his rope getting shorter as it wound around the stake that was banged into the ground. I approached him; he was very friendly but scared, so I stroked his neck and soothed him. Then, taking his halter, I walked him around in the opposite direction, the rope lengthening with each turn, until the rope was at full length and the horse had some grass to graze. This seemed to settle him and I stood back to marvel at him. His coat shone like gold and his flaxen mane was long and flowing, he was a real beauty. I wondered who owned him, vehemently hoping it was not Henrique.

Shortly afterwards, Pedro walked proudly into the yard, I knew him quite well as he dealt with tourism in Góis, and I had been to a few meetings with him.

"What do you think of my horse" he asked proudly.

"He is stunning" I answered meaningfully. "But can you ride?"

"Oh, I can hang on," he laughed. "How hard can it be? Henrique is teaching me."

Doubt spread through my mind. I had kept my horses at this farm for seven years and always been happy, but lately I had been coming home filled with anxiety.

Steve had noticed the change in me. We were both concerned for our horses' safety, how could we run riding holidays when they were not safe? We had not had many enquiries for holidays this year, but had a mother and teenage daughter booked to come for a week's holiday in six weeks time. I just hoped my horses would have recovered from their injuries by then.

That night, we were awoken at 2.30am by bright lights in our driveway and a police horn blowing. Steve stumbled out of bed and went to investigate. Two police officers were standing in our yard; they told us that there were horses on the road in Góis. They wanted us to come, as we were the only address they had of horse owners in the vicinity.

We all drove in convoy to the farm to pick up halters and ropes, and to see which horses were missing. I called to my horses as they had been left out in the field. I hoped that it wasn't them that were running loose around Góis, and after a minute I saw Roxy's white snip on his nose appear out of the darkness. I felt a flush of love as he trotted towards me with his lovely little Welsh ears pricked. Guv, Smartie, Comet and Apollo, followed behind, all very curious.

The policemen were still standing outside the fence under a street light; they were talking amongst themselves and looked a bit edgy. Finally, one of them called to us.

"Could you come and help us please, we don't have any experience with horses." I could see the door of the barn was open, and knew exactly whose horses were running amok in town.

"Yes, of course we will help you." Steve called back, throwing the halters and ropes onto the back seat and getting into our car. We caught the two stallions easily, they were nervous and scared; Henrique's stallion had his head low to the ground, he looked in pain, and I think they were happy for someone to come and take charge. We led them slowly the one kilometre back to the farm; the pregnant mare followed quietly behind us, and the policemen walked ahead of us in the road to slow traffic...although there was none at that time in the morning. We settled the three horses back into their stables, and threw them an armful of hay each, as they had none in their hay ricks. One of the policemen walked back into town to pick up his jeep and we all squeezed in, very grateful for a lift back into town where we had left our car. We were exhausted.

I didn't get a word of thanks from Henrique, but as he told me of his latest plan, my mouth just dropped open! He wanted to bulldoze a big track, zig-zagging over the grazing land; not only to ride horses around, but also for off road motor bike racing. Surely this couldn't be happening; it was too crazy for words. Yet as the digger pulled up outside the gate, I knew that he was serious and I knew we had to get out of there.

CHAPTER 5

THE GREAT WALL OF PORTUGAL

Steve had almost come to blows with Henrique, and the tension between us all was too great, someone had to leave. Sometimes when you find yourself pushed into a corner, it is wise to take a look around that corner, and maybe find a new direction. We had been talking about bringing the horses' home for a while now, it would be so much easier to run our business if the horses were living at our farm with us, instead of three kilometres away.

Steve thought that by taking away a steep sloping bank of grass that separated our house from the road above us, and building a supporting wall, we would have enough room in our yard to build four stables and a hay barn. In the meantime, we had three sheds which could become temporary stables. We had a small field where the horses could have some freedom; it was not what they were used to, but at least they would be safe and maybe we could rent some more land nearby.

We hired machinery to clear away the bank of grass, it almost doubled the size of useable space in our yard, and Steve started building 'The Great Wall of Portugal'. We had a time frame as we had our guests arriving in a month, and we didn't want the yard to look like a building site, so we hired two Portuguese bricklayers to help. Firstly, they laid a foundation of concrete and steel, but the weather forecast was not great, there were storms and rain coming. Steve and the two men managed to lay the first three layers of concrete blocks along the thirty metres of foundation. But the storm arrived early, and the following morning, after a rain lashed night, Steve apprehensively went out to check on his wall. It was not there!

The land above our yard was made of clay and sand. When it was dry, it was as hard as rock, but when it was wet it acted like a bowl of custard. We had unwittingly taken away the grassy bank that had held everything together, and now we were dangerously close to having the road collapse into our yard. It was imperative to build the wall up quickly before that happened. The three men sloshed around in the custardy mud, until the beginnings of the wall were visible again and they could carry on building the wall up higher. We were luckier with the weather, and after the initial catastrophe the retaining wall was soon finished.

We didn't have time to build the stables, but it was early spring so the horses could all live out in our field. They all settled in well and made short work of the grass, but I also had some good hay to keep them happy. The horses had all been to our farm before, in fact Comet and Apollo had been born there. Francisco very kindly said I could use his field which was adjacent to ours to graze the horses; he was not planning on using it this year, and the manure would be good for the soil.

The day arrived for our next guests to visit. Julia and Sarah were mother and daughter and they had booked a week's riding holiday with us. Julia had told us beforehand that she needed to spend more quality time with her daughter Sarah, who was having a few problems; she didn't mention what the problems were.

As soon as Sarah mounted Smartie, I could tell that she was an accomplished rider. She shyly told me she had been riding for ten years and had started when she was just four years old. It was her true passion, and it showed. Smartie, who had been trained in dressage when he was younger, rode beautifully for her. Sarah had lovely light hands and a calm gentle manner. Julia had ridden a lot as a child but now only rode occasionally. She rode Guv, who although he had started his life as a racehorse in Ireland, was a very kind and easy horse to ride.

We all enjoyed our first ride; even Roxy behaved nicely for a change! Later, at lunchtime, Julia asked if Sarah could eat in her bedroom as she was tired. Steve, who had cooked a nice lunch, said that it wouldn't be a problem, he would dish Sarah up a plate of food and she could eat what she wanted. Later when Julia returned the plate, nothing had been eaten. At dinner the same scenario was played and the plate of homemade quiche, baked potato oozing with butter, and mixed salad from the garden came back untouched. We were concerned and asked Julia what foods Sarah liked to eat. Julia asked if we had any crisps. The next day was the same; we tried to offer basic foods like fresh bread rolls, cheese and fruit, but Sarah only ate crisps in her bedroom.

It was strange because while Sarah was riding, she was animated and happy, but as soon as we were home, she went to her room and we hardly saw her for the rest of the day. Steve was concerned, so he spoke to Julia who admitted that she thought Sarah had an eating disorder. She had hoped that coming away on a riding holiday might have distracted her, but that hadn't happened.

She said Sarah was tired and listless except when she was on or around horses. I had noticed that she spent some time with Apollo, my nervous, highly strung youngster. I had started riding him in our field, but he only had a very basic education. I asked Sarah if she would like to ride him. I explained that he had not been schooled so it would be like teaching a baby.

She was thrilled, and that afternoon, after her non-lunch, Sarah didn't stay in her room but spent lots of time grooming and talking to him. Later in the afternoon, when the sun was beginning to sink behind the hills, we led Apollo down into our field, and she rode him for the first time. Apollo was a stunning looking horse; he had been gelded, but still had the proud stance of a stallion. He was a dark dappled grey with an almost white mane and tail; he had a very loving nature and I adored him.

That evening, Sarah was exhausted; we explained that if she wanted to ride Smartie and Apollo daily, she needed fuel—she had to eat.

"Tell me what you would like and I will cook it for you" begged Steve.

"Steak and chips please," came the reply. We were all stunned, including her mother.

"I know I need more energy, and I want to carry on riding, so I will eat steak and chips, if that's okay Steve?"

"Yes of course; no problem," said Steve reaching for the frying pan. "Steak and chips it is!" Our afternoon sessions continued throughout the week. Sarah was incredibly patient with Apollo, just teaching him to walk and stop repeatedly, and always rewarding him with a pat on his neck. They both enjoyed these sessions and as the week went on, Apollo learned to change direction across the field, transition from walk to trot and also to go backwards a couple of steps. Sarah exaggeratedly took off her cardigan, waving her arms around and dragging it across his back and across his neck; this petrified him at first, but with her gentle voice and kind hands, he learned to trust her, and accept what was happening on board his back.

Julia told us that they had booked a week in Lisbon, but if we were able to have them for another week, she would gladly cancel it and stay with us. This was great news for us as we needed the business and Apollo was learning a lot.

During their second week, we started taking Apollo out for short rides. It was a completely new world for him, with so many new sights and sounds. Sarah rode him in the middle of our group, with Julia leading on the wonderful Guv, who gave all the horses such confidence. I brought up the rear on Roxy.

Apollo was so excited, jogging and jumping on the spot, but Sarah just sat quietly—until she sneezed! Apollo shot up in the air in shock! After sneezing and regaining her balance, Sarah needed to blow her nose, so taking one hand off the reins, she reached into her pocket for a tissue, and as quietly as possible she blew into the tissue. Apollo shot forward as if a monster was chasing him, almost concertinaing into Guv's backside, but Guv just walked on quietly, totally ignoring him, and soon Apollo settled into a nice pace.

On another day, we passed under some low branches, which scraped on Sarah's fibreglass riding helmet—Apollo jumped so high that she nearly got caught in the branches of the tree! Sarah was now eating almost normally and coming up to sit at the table with us, mainly because she wanted to chat about Apollo's antics of the day, and also because she had fallen in love with Moppy, and enjoyed playing with her after meals. Too soon, the time came for them to leave; I would miss them, but to my surprise, they booked to come back in the autumn half term.

Rumours started to emerge concerning Henrique. He had bought a lovely old house that needed completely renovating. He had employed a local builder to do the work, who was a very

46

honest, hard worker. We knew Lionel well and he told us that he had not received any money from Henrique for the work he had done so far. He always had an excuse, Lionel told us; he had also heard that although Henrique gave big parties for all of his friends in the local restaurants, he never paid the bill, always saying that he would pay next week, and because he had standing in the town, he was able to get away with it. Now it seemed he had disappeared, leaving unpaid debts all over town. His house was up for sale, and his horses had gone. Although I felt sorry for all Henrique's creditors, especially Lionel, I was happy not to have to see his toady face ever again.

Our good friends Mark and Trish had been away travelling in Mexico. They had spent some weeks volunteering to help baby turtles safely reach the sea, working mainly at night. A wildlife organisation would drop them and other volunteers on the beach and they spent the night scouring the beaches for any signs of life or movement from the many turtle eggs that had been buried by the adult turtles two months before. A female turtle can lay up to 100 eggs, and this particular bay was littered with nests, so it was demanding but incredibly rewarding work.

When as many as possible of the babies had been ushered to the sea, Mark and Trish carried on with their travels. They wanted to explore the mountains, so they bought bus tickets for the long hazardous journey. Here is the account of their journey:

They boarded an old rickety bus and found a seat. The driver was smoking a cigarette while chatting to a pretty girl who was standing next to his cab. Mark and Trish had been told tales of how dangerous this bus route was, with potential landslides and sharp bends with two-way traffic. The road was quite well used by buses and logging trucks, and they became more anxious as the driver answered his phone, talking and laughing as the bus rumbled on. Trish told me later how frightened she had felt as she sat in her seat helpless, while the bus screeched around yet another bend. The young driver was still chatting into his phone, which was tucked between his chin and his shoulder. He was gesticulating with one hand and steering the bus with the other.

She foresaw her doom as the bus skidded off the road and tumbled down a cliff. The driver and the young girl, who had been standing next to his cab, were both killed instantly. Mark was thrown clear but had a branch embedded in his head, and Trish's back was broken. Mark was treated by the emergency ambulance crew that eventually arrived, who managed to pull out the branch cleanly, and after being patched up, Mark recovered completely. Trish had to be airlifted to hospital and after being put into a full body brace, she was driven to the airport by ambulance to be flown back to England; luckily she had taken out good insurance. Despite all of this, she still remembered that she had promised me a bottle of Mexican tequila! She begged the ambulance driver to stop at a shop and buy a bottle of tequila for me; and he did!

I had decided that it was time to start taking Comet out on the road to get him used to all the new sights and sounds. I thought it would be easier, and give Comet more confidence, if I rode Guv and led Comet on the inside of him, so that he could get used to cars, motor bikes, and other road users, while under Guv's protective influence.

I put an old bridle with no reins on Comet, and attached a long rope to the bridle to lead him from. I chose an early Sunday morning when the roads would be extra quiet, and we set off. Things went really well until we came across two 'sleeping policemen' (yellow and black raised rubber strips across the road to slow traffic) set about 20 metres apart.

Comet stopped in trepidation, and after sniffing the rubber, he made a huge leap over, which pulled the rope right out of my hands. I jumped down from Guv, leaving him standing in the middle of the road, and made a grab for the end of the rope: but Comet trod on it just before I reached it and the impact broke the old bridle. Comet was now running around in the middle of the road with nothing on his head and the bridle in tatters, scattered over the road!

Luckily, he was hemmed in by the other 'sleeping policeman' 20 metres away, which he snorted at in horror. He definitely wasn't going to cross that bogeyman: I managed to put the rope around his neck and made a makeshift halter from the rope, then tried to lead both horses back over the sleeping policeman that had caused all of the trouble! Comet refused to budge; he would not cross the monstrous yellow and black rubber strip. Just then, I noticed an old man walking slowly towards us. He had a rolled-up newspaper in his hand and I think he had already summed up the problem. Most of the older people living in these mountain villages are used to dealing with farm animals—donkeys, bullocks, and stubborn goats.

He started waving the rolled-up newspaper and shouting out loud. Comet didn't know which was worse—being attacked by a rubber strip or a shouting newspaper. He opted for the former and jumped back over the sleeping policeman; this time I made sure I held onto the rope! I waved my thanks to the man, who was probably on his way to church...or the bar; whichever one, I'm sure he would proudly regale his story of how he had aided the mad Englishwoman.

I'm sure that this was how a lot of people saw me. I had all these horses that didn't seem to do any work. The villagers saw the horses riding around with tourists on their backs, which to them did not classify as work. Work, to people here in the mountains, meant ploughing or pulling a cart full of produce. There was still a very strong circle of life; most of my neighbours kept goats for milk, cheese and meat. The young male goats would be culled for meat, and also any older female goats would end up on the table once their milking days were over.

One evening when my daughter Mella was staying with us, we went to our local restaurant. We knew the owner well, he had a bizarre sense of humour which Steve appreciated and we'd had some great evenings there. We couldn't make up our minds what to eat; Mella asked the restaurant owner what Chanfana was. He spoke no English, but started making a noise that could have been a goat or a sheep, we were not sure; so, beckoning us into the back room, he opened up the freezer and pulling out a whole goat carcass, he flung it down with a huge bang, onto the metal table. It was so funny to see the look of shock on Mella's face! She didn't have the Chanfana that time, but she has since and really enjoyed the slow braised old goat cooked in red wine and herbs.

A lot of families kept an ox to help with ploughing and general farm work. Once the ox reached a certain age, it would be culled and the family would enjoy the meat for a very long time. One day Francisco asked me in all innocence, "When do you cull the horses, they have excellent meat you know?" I was not shocked, I had been asked this question before, and I could see his point. From his perspective, the horses didn't work, they cost a lot of money to feed, and they would taste so good. I think he was ready to put in his order for some juicy steaks. I tried to explain to him that holidaymakers would pay a lot of money to ride the horses and enjoy Portugal from horseback, so we didn't need to eat them, but he just couldn't understand. Francisco had spent his life growing vegetables and raising animals for the table, to feed his family; he couldn't see the point in just riding something that would taste so good! He took off his flat cap and rubbed his brow, then looking baffled, he shook his head, and walked with a disappointed stoop back to his home.

One thing the locals did like my horses for, was their poo! They would fight over it. When I cleaned the field, I emptied the wheelbarrows of manure onto a pile which grew bigger every day. I told the local community that they could help themselves, but no: they wanted me to divide it up for them so that there would be no arguments. To me, it was a pile of poop, but to them it was like gold. One time I was shopping in the village, and an old lady that I had once given a sack of dung to, shouted out to me,

"Senhora de strum!" (shit woman) raising her hand as she hobbled towards me. Other shoppers turned to see who she was calling to. If a hole had opened up in the ground, I would have jumped in! I felt so embarrassed, but instead I smiled and asked her if she would like another sack of manure. Her toothless face lit up into a big smile. I knew that she had kept goats all her life and their manure would have fed her garden, but now she was too old to keep animals, so my horse poop was really precious to her. I also knew that I would receive a bag of goodies; homemade bread and cakes and of course plenty of cabbage, when I dropped off the gold. I just wished she could remember my name!

CHAPTER 6

OLD PEG TOOTH

We had become friendly with a Dutch couple by the name of Edda and Espen. It was they who had helped us out when Henrique's stallion had injured our horses. They were building a riding business similar to ours, but the difference was that they had capital, whereas we were rather underfunded. They had already built two guest cottages and a swimming pool and were now advertising for holidaymakers for the summer season. They had a lot of bookings and needed to buy some more horses.

They had brought two Dutch warmblood horses with them from Holland and had already bought four Portuguese horses. They were now looking at buying two more young Lusitano horses, and they asked me if I would help train them. We had no riding bookings of our own for the next two months, so I readily agreed to work for them. Steve was busy building our stables, and he had a mate to help him, so I wasn't really needed, and the money I earned working for Edda would help pay for his friend's time.

There was and still is, an organisation known as WWOOF, which stands for willing workers on organic farms. It's a great organisation and gives opportunities to anyone, but mainly students, to travel the world and work on farms in different locations. In return they get board and lodgings and sometimes some pocket money. Our friends Mark and Trish had originally come to Portugal through the WWOOF organisation where they volunteered on a farm way up in the mountains. The farm proved to be a bit too isolated for them as they were both gregarious people, and eventually they found a job working with mentally and physically challenged people near to the Serra da Estrela mountain range. They were responsible for the wellbeing of a group of six adults, which included expanding their minds and bodies with activities, and this was how we had originally met them some years before.

Trish had noticed our horses on her way into town one morning, and had stopped to ask me if they could bring their group for riding lessons. We readily agreed and although it would be a challenge, we were looking forward to meeting the group that consisted of five men and one lady called Ana. Ana had a true love of animals and was happy just to stand next to Comet and stroke his neck; then she would smell her hands and smile. She also loved to pet our dogs, and Bica would always run to Ana when she arrived, wagging her tail at the prospect of being spoilt. Paolo, one of the men, had something wrong with his balance, and would just tumble over without any warning; hence he needed to be held by two people at all times. He desperately wanted to ride a horse, but getting him up there was definitely going to be a challenge.

Steve built a huge mounting block out of an old table top, and added steps to climb up on top of it. Paolo and Mark and Trish climbed up onto the table top, and they both pushed and bolstered Paolo up onto Guv's back. Steve stood on the other side of Guv so that Paolo didn't fall straight off again. Guv stood stock still through the whole procedure, as if he understood what was happening, and Paolo almost exploded with delight. Mark and Trish walked on each side of him, holding on to his legs as Guv slowly walked a few steps. Amazingly his balance on a moving horse was good and as long as he didn't lose concentration, his lessons went really well; the look on his face made all the effort worthwhile. All of the group loved the horses and always brought a bag of chopped carrots and apples to feed them, not minding at all the frothy saliva that ended up all over their hands.

Sadly, after many months of getting to know these lovely people, Mark and Trish left the job and bought their small farm where Foxy had spent some time last winter, before I sold her. The next people employed to look after the group didn't want the responsibility of bringing them riding. On the group's last visit, Paolo and Ana both cried, and everyone in the group brought me home-made presents and cards; it was a very sad day for all of us.

Edda had applied to the WWOOF organisation for an experienced horse volunteer, and was expecting a young English girl to come and stay on her farm, to help with the horses. Libby arrived the following week, and it was apparent straight away that she was very experienced with horses. The two new horses had been delivered, one was a stunning bright bay with a long black mane and tail called Rouxinal which translates as Nightingale; and the other was a grey mare called Palmeira, which translates as Palm tree.

Rouxinal was to be my project, he was so beautiful, I couldn't wait to get to know him and ride him. Edda and Espen's farm was about half an hour's drive from us, and I arranged to go over three times a week to lunge and school Rouxinal, and also ride two of the other horses to help get them fit for the coming season. I really enjoyed the work, it was nice to be around horsey people again, and I loved Rouxinal, he was so gentle and easy to teach.

The young horses needed to be ridden outside of the farm to experience traffic and all of the different sights and sounds that they would come across in the mountains. Edda decided that it would be a safe option to ride one of the young horses in the middle of two of the more experienced ones, so on a fine spring morning, Edda, Libby and I set out together, with me riding Rouxinal in the middle of the group. I breathed in the ineffably sweet aromas from all the fruit blossoms and wild flowers that we passed on our way, it felt so good to be alive and riding this wonderful high stepping horse. Rouxinal behaved well, he was going to be a real asset to Edda's business.

On the next occasion, Edda wanted Libby to ride one of the other horses that had been having a few problems. He had been bucking, and we needed to get him out of the habit before the first guests arrived. Edda hoped that more work would be the best answer for him. I was glad that it was Libby riding the bucking bronco, and that I would have a nice easy ride on the rather lazy young mare Palmeira

But, oh no! It was her first ride outside of the arena and she was very skittish. We saw a donkey and cart ahead, coming slowly down a steep tarmac hill, which was bordered on our side by an old clay pit quarry. The wheels of the cart had ancient metal rims which made a loud noise on the tarmac. Palmeira stopped dead in the middle of the road; she was terrified and I could feel her whole body shaking under me. The donkey slowly walked towards us, a wizened old man was sitting up on the cart waving his stick gently with every few strides that the donkey took. He had no idea of the drama that they were about to create.

Palmeira reared right up high: as she landed she tried to turn and run back down the tarmac hill. I couldn't let her do that, but as the donkey came closer and the metal wheels got louder, she reared a second time. She was now dangerously close to the edge of a sheer drop into a quarry. I tried to turn her but she reared again, and this time she overbalanced and crashed to the ground missing the sheer drop by inches, and with me still on her back! My leg was stuck under her as she thrashed to get back up, and I remember fleetingly thinking "Oh my god, my leg must be broken." Miraculously it wasn't, and I managed to throw my feet out of the stirrups and jump off, as the panic-stricken horse struggled to her feet.

The old man and the donkey plodded on past us; they hadn't even realised that they had been the cause of the accident. Edda, who had been trying to alert the old man, shouting for him to stop, jumped down from her horse and after checking that I was ok, she held on to poor Palmeira who was still very nervous, while I brushed myself off and re-mounted her.

Once back at Edda's farm, I took off my boot which had become very tight. I watched my ankle visibly swell once it was released from the boot. Edda told me to go and sit by the pool and dangle my leg into the cold water, which gave instant relief. After a few minutes soaking, I could move my ankle in both directions, so we all agreed that it was a bad sprain and not broken. It was very painful though, yet at the time of the accident, it hadn't really hurt. I guess it was all the adrenaline that coursed through my body and blocked the pain. I would need to rest my ankle for a few weeks, so no more riding for me!

Normally Craig cycled the four kilometres to school, but if he was late or if the weather was inclement, I would take him in the car. It was a stunning journey, through narrow roads bordered by rich woodland which rose up to a hilltop village that seemed to be permanently in the sun. From this hilltop village, we had wonderful views over the surrounding land, and as we dropped down into the town of Góis, we passed a tumbledown house which stood alone.

An old couple lived there without sanitation or electricity. The old man was as thin as a beanpole, very scruffy and leant heavily on his stick. I think he had Parkinson's disease, because he wobbled as he walked and his left hand that was not supported by his stick shook alarmingly. He only had one tooth so as we did not know his name, he became known as 'Peg Tooth' to us. His wife Rosa was always dressed in multiple layers of old worn out clothes, and was usually toiling in the large garden.

Old Peg Tooth would walk two kilometres into Góis, wildly swaying back and forth across the thankfully quiet roads, carrying an empty 5 litre wine bottle and return later with a very red face and an even more ungainly gait carrying a full 5 litres of wine. Rosa often walked up the very steep hill to the village where her sister lived so if we were passing her house in our car, we always offered her a lift up the steep hill. She was so sweet, and always wanted to give us something in return, so on one occasion when we had given her a lift down the hill back to her home, she asked if we would like some oranges.

She had a huge tree in her garden, and we all loved oranges, so we accepted gratefully. Steve went towards the ladder which was positioned against the orange tree, with an empty shopping bag, thinking that he would climb the rickety ladder and fill the bag, but Rosa, who must have been at least seventy years old, ran in front of him, and pushing him aside, proceeded to climb the ladder. Steve tried to protest, but she would hear none of it, and she passed us down lovely juicy oranges until our bag was full.

One day I noticed bruises on her face, but she said she had been butted by one of her goats, so I thought no more of it. Then a few weeks later, we were riding the horses past their house, when she came running out, with Peg Tooth chasing after her, brandishing his stick. Luckily, she could easily outrun him, and she signalled to us that she didn't need any help. She seemed to accept his actions as normal. When I asked if she was ok, she brushed the whole incident off, saying that he just got a bit silly when he was drunk, but I was still worried for her safety. Then one day we saw a hearse parked outside their house, and I feared the worst. Shortly afterwards, Rosa appeared dressed all in black; it was Peg Tooth that had died.

Not long afterwards, the tumbledown house took on a transformation. It seemed that Peg Tooth had not had a bank account, but had stashed big wads of money under his mattress. Rosa now lives in comfort, she had a bathroom installed and electricity connected. She still climbs her rickety ladder to pick oranges and olives from her garden, and still walks up the steep hill to visit her sister, so her hard life seemed to have done her no lasting harm.

During the summer, as my ankle improved, I swam every afternoon. I would muck out and feed the horses, then walk down our track to the river bank, and emerge myself into the cool deep water, then laze on the veranda, in my hammock...ah bliss. Life was very different for Edda; she had advertised her new riding holidays widely in Holland and had many guests arriving. She still had Libby working for her with the horses, and had taken on a cook and a cleaner. Although she had help, Edda was showing signs of stress.

Espen, her husband, was not really cut out for dealing with the general public; he would shut himself away with his new computer, leaving the running of the business to Edda. The swimming pool leaked, and there were numerous problems with the newly built guest accommodation; I felt sorry for her, but at least she was making money which was more than we were! Once her holidays were fully booked, she passed on our information to potential clients wanting to come on a riding holiday in Portugal. This was quite lucrative for us, and we were very grateful.

We were now preparing to meet a Dutch couple who had been sent to us by Edda for a riding holiday.

Noah and Amalia were a middle-aged couple who both spoke excellent English. They were both good riders and very nice company. Amalia was an endurance rider and loved Arabs, so she immediately clicked with Smartie. Noah was a very tall, elegant man, so he was perfectly matched with my thoroughbred Guv. As they were both experienced riders, I had decided to ride Apollo; it would be his first full week of work, and I hoped to ride him in the lead. Both Noah and Amalia assured me that if there were any problems, they would be happy to take the lead which gave me the confidence I needed.

The first day's ride took us through eucalyptus and pine forest which led to a very remote village; we then had to ford a river, which was only about half a metre deep, but Apollo had never done it before. Noah splashed through first on Guv, followed by Amalia on Smartie. Apollo, not wanting to be left alone on the other side of the river, teetered for a moment and then leaped into the water to catch up with his friends, drenching me in the process! I think he surprised himself with his bravery, and I was very proud of him. I liked to do this particular ride on a Sunday when there would not be much traffic, because we came back home through a larger town, where I could point out various shops and cafes that our guests might like to visit during their stay.

We generally offered three morning rides, leaving the guests free to enjoy the river or to go out exploring in the afternoons. On the other two days, we took people on picnic day rides. Steve would drive to the picnic spots and set up a delicious lunch for us; most of our picnic locations were by a river so that we could take a swim and cool off before the long ride home.

I was really looking forward to riding Apollo on his first picnic experience; he was such a pleasure to ride, although still a little spooky. We were heading for a gorge, where the river flowed deep and slow through sheer sided rock which was at least 30 metres high. There was a man-made weir which held the water back and created a pool. I had been bringing guests to this lovely spot for a while, and although there were sometimes other people there, it was generally very quiet, so imagine my surprise as we approached the gorge with rumbling tummies, dreaming of the delights that Steve had brought for us, to hear blaring trance music echoing through the mountains.

Guv and Smartie hardly changed stride as they rounded a corner and surveyed the scene, they were used to encountering brass bands and blaring music when we passed through villages holding their annual festivals, but Apollo had never seen or heard anything like the sight that now met our eyes. A rave party had obviously taken place on the night before; the music was still pounding and some people were still dancing. There was a man lying stretched out on the pathway that we were walking on. Guv and Smartie walked carefully around him, but Apollo just didn't know how to react. I tried to steer him around but he panicked and leapt over the man who seemed to be in a hallucinogenic state.

"Wow man," I heard him say, "I just saw a flying horse!"

There was a field a little further down the gorge where the horses could eat some grass, and we would be tucked away from the party. Luckily just at that moment, the music stopped; they had run out of fuel for their generator. I could still hear the booming sound ringing in my ears for a minute before the sounds of running water and nature returned. The party broke up once the music stopped, and soon we had the area to ourselves to enjoy our picnic and swim in the wonderful deep water created by the narrow gorge.

As we swam, the sunlight chased the reflection of our ripples and sent them shimmering up the smooth face of the rock. Afterwards we sat on rocks with our feet cool in the water and watched crag martins and swallows skim the water as they chased insects, while wagtails hunted in the long, lush grass growing around the edges of the pool for baby frogs. With frog's legs dangling from their beaks, they would fly to the nearest rock, and smash their poor prey onto the hard surface. I saw a movement in the grass near to where I was sitting, it was a grub, some kind of larva, wriggling on a blade of grass. We all sat mesmerized for a time by this creature that was gradually emerging before our eyes into a beautiful dragon fly. It slowly opened its reflective wings until they were quite dry; then it flew off into the throng of other flying insects and birds that made their life in this beautiful natural environment. A strange and awe-inspiring day.

CHAPTER 7

WWOOFERS

After meeting Libby at Edda's farm, and learning about the WWOOF organisation, we decided to join ourselves. We were asked by the organisation to write a description of our farm, and what we could offer volunteers in the way of accommodation and food. The organisation also wanted to know what type of work we would be expecting volunteers to help us with. Steve needed help with lots of small building and gardening projects, and I would always be grateful for any help in looking after the horses.

The first person to apply to our post was an 18 year old French/Canadian lad called François, from Quebec. He was travelling Europe, and was in France helping out in a community set up by a British couple who were trying to promote raw food diets. He would be leaving them in a few weeks and would like to come to Portugal...and eat some hot food!

The arrangements were all made, and we were looking forward to him arriving, and staying with us for the month of September. A few days later, we had a desperate phone call from François, begging to come earlier...straight away! He was phoning from a public phone, so he couldn't explain, but we readily agreed. Steve picked him up from the bus station, and my first impression, as he unfolded from our little old Renault van, was what a handsome young man he was. François was tall and lean, with blonde dreadlocks trailing down his back and striking blue eyes, shaded by long lashes that made me envious.

After settling him into the caravan, I made some coffee and we all sat and chatted. He told us that at first he had enjoyed working and learning about the benefits of raw food, foraging daily for food, and living a very minimalistic lifestyle. However, the couple running the retreat had a very open relationship, and not long after his arrival, the woman's desires became fixated on him. She followed him, trying to get him alone, and although he dodged her as best he could, she eventually cornered him in his tent, and made very strong advances towards him: he fled, and made the desperate call to us. Craig arrived home from school, and he and François instantly became friends, sharing music and skateboarding stories. For an 18 year old, he had done an awful lot in his life, but for the moment, he was happy to have a cooked meal, and a safe bed to sleep!

The first soft September rains fell at dawn; the pattering of raindrops on our palm tree through my open bedroom window awoke me. I padded barefoot out onto my patio and took in the smell of the air. I wish I could send through these pages the fragrant bouquet that accosted me. The summer dried forest floor was releasing its stored aromas from the dampened earth; rich musty scents, mixed with pine resin, and the strong smell of eucalyptus bark that lay scattered on the ground: it was like receiving an aromatherapy hit! We needed this rain, but alas, it was just a brief shower, teasing the trees and my veggie garden. All too soon dawn gave way to golden beams of morning sun, that steadily slid down from the hilltop to flood our valley with their warmth.

François was up early, and ready to work, he had brought us a bottle of maple syrup from his hometown, so I made pancakes for breakfast. Afterwards, Craig left for school, and Steve and François set themselves up to carry on building 'the great wall of Portugal.' Steve had already built wooden stables along most of the wall, but the last section would be visible within our garden, and we wanted to build it out of stone rather than concrete blocks.

François had a little experience with building work, but he had never worked with stone before and was keen to try his hand. At first, he searched and selected good rocks to use, while Steve built the wall. We had an endless supply of rocks because of the tumbledown ruins that we had recently bought, and as time went on, François proved to be a quick learner with an artistic eye. Steve was soon able to leave him alone to build the stone wall while he started another project, which would be building a concrete walk-way outside the stables. Horses are notoriously good at attracting mud, and the area outside the stables was often stodgy with mud. A wide concrete walkway would help a lot, and be easy to sweep clean.

Halfway through the job, Steve's trusty old cement mixer clattered to a halt: the main bearing had broken. Our local garage said that they could repair it for us, but we had to get it to them. It was only a two kilometre journey, but the mixer only had two wheels on the front; the back of the mixer had a strong leg over the drum, which you could use to lift it off the ground to push it short distances around a building site; but not that sort of distance and there was no way it would fit in our old Renault Express van. Ever optimistic, Steve and François lifted the wheels into the van, and pushed it as far back as they could. It was only about halfway in, when François had a brain wave.

"Could we have a plank sticking out of the back of the van to sit the rest of the mixer on?"

"That's a great idea," mused Steve, thoughtfully rubbing his chin. So the mixer came back out of the van, and a long strong plank was put in. Then they lifted the wheels back into the van, straddling the plank. Next they lifted the leg at the back of the mixer up onto the plank which hung outside of the van, and of course the plank see-sawed under the weight.

"Why don't you sit on the front of the plank?" Steve joked.

"Ok," laughed François, "Sounds fun"

Now a Renault Express was only a small van, the back was only about 1.5 metres high and François was a big lad. He squeezed awkwardly past the mixer and into the back of the van, and pushing the plank down, he sat dubiously on it with his head bowed down and his shoulders touching the roof. Steve hooked a bungee onto the back doors, and they set off precariously up the drive. The whole contraption started to slip backwards, and I could see a look of trepidation cross François's face, as he clung to the front seats of the van while keeping his weight firmly on the plank.

"Don't worry," chuckled Steve from the relative safety of the driver's seat, "there's no more hills from now on…. I'll try not to hit any bumps in the road, the front end feels so light I think I could pull a wheelie!" François muttered something under his breath in

French; I think he was regretting his brain wave, but they managed to reach the garage without further hitches, and when the cement mixer was fixed, they had to do the whole journey in reverse!

François stayed with us for two months, before setting off on a new adventure. The following spring, we welcomed a young girl from California. She had been helping out on a horse ranch in Spain, and I was looking forward to her helping me to get our horses fit for the coming season. Her name was Pye, and she was a dog groomer from California, which I was really pleased to hear, because we had three dogs, and they all needed some pampering. Moppy was half poodle, she didn't shed any hair, which obviously had advantages, but it did mean that I had to give her a haircut at least twice a year, and at that moment, she was very shaggy. Bica was half collie, and shed enough hair for all three of them, so she always needed a good brushing, and Toby was just a big friendly Labrador who loved being spoilt!

Pye was a slight, pretty girl with short light brown hair and striking almond eyes; she had a confident air that made her seem older than her 21 years. She was a good rider with a sunny disposition, which was soon noticed by Adam, our nearest English neighbour. He suddenly showed an interest in riding my horses, and asked Pye to give him some riding lessons in our arena. I could hear her giggling at his attempts to trot; I think she liked him too.

We had our first guests of the year at Easter time; they were a family with a 12 year old daughter. One day whilst out riding, we came across a huge fallen Mimosa tree, it was much too high to step over but too low to ride under. I thought that if we all dismounted and led the horses, they would just about fit under the tree. When we were all on the other side, we mounted the horses and prepared to set off. Pye was riding Roxy and had been the last one to go under the tree. She put her foot in the stirrup and was almost mounted, when Roxy spun around, and galloped back towards the fallen tree. There was no way that Pye could fit under the tree, we were all watching in horror, unable to do anything, when she threw her arms up into the air and grabbing a branch of the tree, she swung in mid-air as Roxy disappeared underneath. She jumped lightly down onto the ground like a circus performer, and took a bow as we all clapped her. Roxy of course, realising that he was on his own and the game was over, came trotting back under the tree. I hopped off of Apollo, and held Roxy's reins for her so that she could mount without any more circus tricks. Pye was on high alert for the rest of the ride, and Roxy knew it, so he begrudgingly behaved himself.

Adam asked Pye if she would like to go for a ride on his motor bike which she accepted excitedly. He had two bikes, one was the type of bike that you ride off-road, on tracks, it was only built to carry one person, but if she held on tight, Adam thought she could just about ride pillion. The other was a big shiny Harley Davison with a very comfortable padded seat. Pye wanted to go off-road and up into the mountains, which I thought was very brave of her, as the tracks were rocky and difficult to negotiate, especially two up on a bike that was only meant to carry one person!

Steve and I often used to work out new routes for our horse rides by learning them first on his bike. Steve's dirt bike had a double seat, so it was more comfortable than Adam's bike, and we often set off for the day, to plan out new rides for me to take guests on. I would take a pocket of string or sometimes a can of spray paint, and tie a piece of string around a tree so that I would know where to turn off of one track and onto another when riding it by horse. It was embarrassing to make mistakes and go the wrong way when leading guests on horseback, but very easy to lose my way in the thick forests. These pieces of string or a blotch of paint on a tree gave me confidence that I was heading in the right direction. Normally going out on the bike was fun, and I enjoyed these missions, but on one disastrous day, we hit a slimy muddy patch of track, and the bike skidded, shot forward and ended up in a bog hole. We were both thrown straight off the back of the bike and I landed on my back like a tortoise, in thick stodgy mud. Steve had a softer landing; he landed on top of me!

Luckily Adam rode very carefully, and Pye didn't fall off, in fact, she came back exhilarated and full of wonder at the beauty of the mountains. Another evening, we were sitting out on the veranda with our guests, when Adam called around on his Harley. He asked Pye if she would like to go to the beach with him, she accepted shyly

"There will be a full moon later," he said.

"Oh, how romantic," our guest whispered to me; "to be lying on a beach with the full moon shining down." Needless to say, we didn't see Pye again until the following day. She saw Adam a few more times, and I think they planned to stay in touch, but she would soon be leaving us to fly to New Zealand, where she was going into the mountains to be a shepherd for 6 months. She would be living in a caravan, alone with just a dog and a horse for company. The cowboys would come every few weeks and move her caravan and help her herd the sheep to a new pasture: what an adventure! She told us that it had seemed like a great idea at the time, but now she was feeling apprehensive about the trip.

We wished her good luck, I would miss her, and so would my doggies, but we were expecting a young French couple called Lyam and Sophia to join us for two weeks. Sophia, who spoke good English, was a horse rider and would be helping me, while Lyam would be helping Steve with odd jobs around the farm. Sophia was a good rider, she taught Comet and Apollo to jump obstacles. Comet was a natural, he really enjoyed it, but Apollo didn't find it so easy, and became nervous and jittery; he would canter sideways up to the obstacle, and then throw in a huge leap, as if the pole was going to bite him! Sophia thought it would be best to just trot him over poles on the ground to start with, and build up slowly as his confidence grew.

Lyam didn't speak any English, and our French was only from long ago schooldays, but it's amazing how a language can come back to you when necessary. Steve actually became quite good at conversing with Lyam as they worked together. He enjoyed the challenge, and Lyam learnt a bit of English, as well as helping us to get a few more jobs ticked off of our ever-growing list!

CHAPTER 8

DUKE

Some very sad news came our way as summer slowly advanced into autumn, and nature threw down its blanket of colour. Our dear friend Edda had been diagnosed with cancer. I knew that she had been treated for breast cancer in the past, but this time the cancer was more invasive and she had already made the decision to return to Holland for treatment. Her two children had never really settled in Portugal and her husband wasn't able to give her the support that she needed, so the whole family were re-locating; Edda, quite understandably, wanted to be near to her parents.

The farm and all of the horses would be sold in due course. Libby would stay on for the time being, to look after the horses. She had already bought Rouxinal (lucky thing!) and she would eventually take him back to England with her.

Edda asked me if I would buy Duke; her favourite horse. He was a stunning golden chestnut Dutch Warmblood with the most wonderful floating trot. I had ridden him a few times and knew he would be good for our business, but as usual, funds were tight. She assured me that money was not an issue; she just wanted me to have him, because she knew he would be safe and that I would look after him. She had owned him since he was weaned and had brought him over from Holland with her. He had been part of her family, but now she must let him go. She was more or less telling me then that she didn't think she would survive this time, and sadly she was right, she died less than a year later.

We didn't have a stable for Duke, so he went to live in the cottage which now had the walls built up, a concrete ring beam poured, then another floor added, making a large mezzanine bedroom. Francisco had offered us one of his eucalyptus trees to use for the main roof ridge beam, it was huge and had taken six of us to lift it, plus two more men who happened to be passing by on a tractor and offered their help. We were very grateful for their kindness as I'm not sure we would have managed to lift it into place without them. We were even more grateful when one of the men told us that he had just re-roofed his house and had thousands of the old style roof tiles to give away. They were exactly the same as the ones on the roof of our house so they would match perfectly.

Our Belarusian friends had left us the year before, because our money had run out, but now they were back to help us put on the roof so that Duke would have a dry place to live. We were so pleased with their work, the kitchen and bathroom partition walls were up, and the floor was concreted; but basically the cottage was a shell with a roof, we had done no rendering and there were no windows, just holes in the brickwork. The kitchen was a perfect Duke sized stable, and that was where he lived for the next few months. He befriended Comet and Apollo, almost becoming a father figure to them; when all the horses were turned out in our paddock, he would herd those two away from the others, but Comet and Apollo didn't seem to mind and they could often be seen scratching each other's backs with their teeth.

Our three dogs all got on well with the horses, Toby was 12 years old, Bica was 7 years old, and our tiny Moppy was one year old. She only weighed about 4 kilos, and looked just like a cute little puppy, yet she had a very strong personality and always managed to secure herself the most comfortable armchair. Toby had always come with me on rides, even in England; he and Roxy were old mates and had shared many adventures over the years. He was now getting old, and although I still took him with me on shorter rides, he had to stay behind on longer trips.

Bica also loved to accompany me when I went riding. She had once been a great help when Apollo came across his first big puddle. It stretched right across the track and had an oily black sheen caused by all the eucalyptus oil in the forest. I was riding Apollo on my own with just Bica for company. He stopped at the puddle and refused to go through because the oily sheen acted like a mirror, and he could see his reflection! I sat patiently in the saddle, urging him forward but he just kept backing away from the puddle and snorting in fear. After a few minutes, Bica, who had been watching intently, walked into the puddle and lay down to cool off. Apollo's ears twitched forward as if a light had been switched on in his brain, "Ah, that's what it is…just water." I felt his confidence return as he tentatively picked his way through the puddle. I was thankful to Bica although I wasn't looking forward to brushing off her mud caked coat when we got home.

When we went on day rides I preferred to not take any dogs with me, especially if the weather was hot. Bica took exception to this and would hide under the caravan until we were all mounted and walking out of the gate, then she would spring out and run on ahead. It was too much hassle to catch her and turn back for home, so she usually got her own way and came with us. If it was too hot by the afternoon, she could always come home in the car with Steve, who always brought us a picnic lunch on our day rides.

During the winter months when we had no guests, I would take out two horses on my own. There was a nice circular ride of 45 minutes that I would use to keep them fit and happy, riding one horse and leading the other. All three dogs would come with me, even little Mop. I really loved these rides with all my animals. We would pass through an old, abandoned village where fields that would have grown crops were now turned over to lush grass.

There was an orange orchard that still gave fruit but there was nobody living there to pick it. The village was totally deserted; there were about six houses still standing, but most of the windows and doors had rotted away so that I could peep inside and see old forgotten furniture that had been abandoned. Brambles were now encroaching, and soon the whole village would disappear from sight under the mass of greedy brambles that were devouring it year by year.

The horses loved this ride because I always stopped and let them eat grass for a while; this gave the dogs a chance to rest, and me to fill my saddle bags with oranges. I had never known anywhere to be so quiet; apart from birdsong, and the happy munching of the horses, the whole village was eerily silent. I asked Francisco if he knew why the village was abandoned, and he told me that the waterfall that had fed the village had dried up when the whole area around it was planted with eucalyptus trees. Eucalyptus put down exceptionally long tap roots, which is why they can grow in very dry areas; they consume water from the water table way underground, leaving the area dry and desolate. Over the years, the waterfall had dried up, and the people had all left. It's a sad fact, but there are many villages just like this one, all over Portugal; the soil is robbed of all its moisture and goodness by the eucalyptus trees, and our need for paper, which is what the trees are grown for.

Our three cats, BB, a huge fat ginger, Robin, a very pretty white cat with ginger markings, and Misty who was tri-coloured, all got on well with the dogs, except when BB tried to steal the dog's dinners! He would crawl between Toby's front paws and steal his food from his dish. Toby stood over him growling and showing his fangs, but BB would ignore him and carry on gorging, totally unfazed. He had always done it, ever since we had found him as a starving little kitten. He was a born thief, but had managed not to use up all of his nine lives just yet!

Robin loved water, he would come down to the river with us and although he wouldn't swim, he would paddle on the edge and wait for us to return from our swim. He loved to try to catch the thousands of baby fish swimming near to the edge, dabbing at them with his paw.

Misty was my favourite cat; she was so sweet and loved to lay in my hammock with me. She had the most beautiful eyes that really seemed to look into my soul, and she would purr as we gently swung in the breeze.

Winter was approaching and Steve had booked a ticket to return to England to work for two long months. We needed the money to continue our work on the cottage. It was just a shell at the moment with a horse living in residence! It needed plumbing, electricity, windows, doors and much more, before we could offer it as guest accommodation. I was dreading Steve leaving, so I was pleased when I had an unexpected phone call from Sophie, an old friend of mine.

We had known each other since our schooldays; her love life had always been a disaster. She was pregnant at the age of seventeen from a one night stand that she never saw again, and to this day the father doesn't know that he has a child. The baby, a beautiful boy, was brought up by Sophie's mother until Sophie married a soldier and moved with him and her son to Germany. Sophie was not suited to army life; she became depressed and dissatisfied, and after five years of marriage, the couple were divorced. Sophie returned with her son to live with her long-suffering mother.

She bought a horse and our friendship rekindled as I was keeping my horse at the same livery stables near Brighton. We spent many hours riding together and catching up on our relationship. I was very happy to have her back in my life, and realised how much I had missed her. Sophie had always been attractive to the opposite sex; with her long lustrous auburn hair and cat like green eyes, she seemed to ooze sex appeal.

Johnny, a big burly farmer who farmed the land next to our livery stables, normally kept himself to himself, yet I began to notice that he always seemed to be on hand whenever Sophie needed a bale of hay lifting or a wheelbarrow of manure emptied. Sure enough, she soon confided in me that she had been flirting with him and he had asked her to go for a drink. He was married with two young children but despite that, they had a passionate affair. She would tell me all the details when we rode together. She was so happy yet I couldn't help but feel sorry for his wife and family who knew nothing of what was going on. After a few months, Johnny cooled and ended their relationship and a heartbroken Sophie moved her horse to another livery yard, so although we still met socially, we didn't see so much of each other.

I hadn't seen or heard from her since my move to Portugal seven years before, yet when she phoned me, it was as if we had never been apart. We were both lonely; Steve had just left for England and would be gone for two months, and Sophie had just come out of what sounded like a horrendous relationship.

"I'll jump on a plane" she said spontaneously; "and come to keep you company."

Craig was a young teenager; his friends were going to Morocco for a month with their family and had invited him to go with them. It would be a great experience for him, but I had been dreading being all alone in the middle of a forest, with just lots of animals for company, but now I had something to look forward to. We would have so much fun. Craig left for Morocco the day before Sophie arrived.

I was shocked when she stepped from the train, she looked frail and vulnerable and much too thin. Sophie had been such a bouncy positive girl, yet I couldn't believe how pale she looked.

I felt the need to play down my happy life, although we had it pretty tough physically, with the struggle to build a life for ourselves on a very limited budget, emotionally Steve and I were rock solid. We had experienced so many adventures, and met so many new friends along the way, and apart from the fact that Steve had to keep going back to England to work, we loved everything about our new life.

Over the next few weeks, Sophie and I talked, drank wine, rode the horses and drank more wine! I could see her mojo returning visibly as she played with the dogs and cats and went searching for duck eggs. She became the cook of the house, and she loved to visit markets to see the different fruit and veggies available.

She talked a lot about her traumatic past and her very controlling second husband, Daniel. She told of how her son, who was now in his twenties, rarely visited her. He had hated his stepfather and had left home as soon as he could. Daniel had also driven a wedge between her and her mother, whom she now rarely saw.

One time when Sophie had planned to go out with friends, Daniel had become so furious that he ran out of the house after her, grabbed the car keys from her hand and threw them into the road where they were driven over by a car that was passing. Now she had escaped and she vowed never to go back.

One day Sophie went to a nearby market town to buy our groceries; when she returned she said that she had met an English man, his name was David. He had asked her to go for a coffee with him and it seemed that they had a lot in common. She had invited him home tonight for dinner. She hoped I didn't mind. I didn't; I was pleased for her and we both looked forward to a nice evening.

David seemed nice, he was older than I had expected and had been a lawyer in New York. He had taken early retirement and moved to Portugal for the climate and a quieter lifestyle. Sophie seemed relaxed and happy in his company; her effervescent personality reappeared as she spent more and more time with him. However, I was shocked when after only three weeks she told me she was moving in with him! It was a real whirlwind romance. I tried to slow her down a bit but she was adamant, saying that she had nothing holding her to England, her mother and her son had their own lives, which didn't include her, so why should she not take a chance on happiness. I just hoped that happiness was what she would find.

A lady phoned me from Ireland saying that she had some time off and would like to come for a riding holiday next week. I couldn't turn away a week's work, but I would be on my own. I asked Sophie if she could help me for a few days, but she said she and David were going away on holiday. She did however cook up a couple of her delicious recipes for me to freeze, which would help me out a lot.

I drove to Lisbon, which was a six hour round trip, to pick up Grace from the airport; she was a very nice lady who had taken up riding quite late in life. Grace was 50 years old and had been riding for 10 years. She mainly rode at a dressage yard and only hacked out on holidays. I had partnered her with Duke and was sure she would like him, as he had been well trained in dressage when he was younger, and was a superb horse to ride.

Grace had been on riding holidays all over the world and I really enjoyed hearing about all of her adventures as we rode every day in the warm December sunshine. One day we were riding down a very narrow track that I hadn't used in many months, and a big strong bramble had looped across the track and taken root on the other side. I was riding Smartie in the lead; he stopped at the obstruction, but I pushed him on, asking him to use his weight to nudge the bramble out of the way. Then I realised that it had rooted firmly, and had evil sharp prickles that were sticking into poor Smartie's neck. I broke a small branch from a tree above my head, and tried to whack the bramble, but this just upset Smartie and he started backing away, thinking I was trying to hit him. This in turn upset Duke, who was waiting patiently behind, and he threatened to rear.

The path was much too narrow to turn around on, or even dismount safely, so I instinctively leant forward over Smartie's neck, and holding the bramble between its evil thorns with two fingers, I bit into its flesh and gnawed, until finally it broke in two. Grace was impressed, and christened us 'the wild women'. She told me some unnerving tales of her riding adventures in Africa where she often came face to face with wild animals; how exciting, but it made my bramble experience seem a little dull.

On another of our rides, through the ancient town of Góis, a Portuguese couple asked us if they could take some pictures of us and the horses which we agreed to. They were very friendly, and introduced themselves as Mario and Anna. They had a holiday home nearby and were staying there for the Christmas holidays. They asked us if we would like to go to dinner at their house the next day. They lived way up in the mountains in a very remote village that I had never visited, but Mario promised to meet us at the turn off from the main road, so that we could follow him for the last few kilometres.

As we rode the horses home, in the low winter sunshine which sent long shadows onto the dank decomposing leaf litter on the forest floor, we made up scenarios, giggling about how our evening could unfold. Who knew what sinister eerie events could take place in a remote mountain village? We scared ourselves so much that we decided to take Toby, my big black dog with us!

Next afternoon, we drove to the top of the range which was at about 800 metres altitude; the sky was blue; the air was warm and windless. Already the sun was slowly sliding down towards the mountains that would engulf it's warmth within the hour. We were a little early, so we parked the car and stood breathing in the wonderful clear air. Toby bounded away, happy at his unexpected freedom. The view was enthralling; hills and valleys stretched out as far as the eye could see. Cloud was beginning to snake through the valleys, and we could see smoke rising from distant hilltop chimneys. There had been no winter frosts yet, and underfoot late blooming heather gave off its sweet smell. Purple ground orchids carpeted the slopes, and a sprawling hypericum bush still had a few bright yellow blooms that turned their faces to the sun.

Mario's wing mirror glinted in the light as he approached to lead us down into his valley. I called to Toby; his ears shot up at the sound of my voice, and although he had picked up a scent and was halfway down the hillside, he galloped back up the hill in easy loping bounds, tongue lolling out, and jumped nimbly into the car. We followed Mario's Land Rover down and down through thickly forested winding roads, where the sun's weak winter rays could not penetrate. The road became a track; on we went, the forest was almost dark even though it was only 3pm. There was a blanket of mist that seemed to be rising from the undergrowth giving the forest a spectral presence, and as we entered Mario's village, we were immersed in thick fog, and could barely see Mario's brake lights as they flickered on. The temperature had plummeted.

"Let's get inside, the fire is alight." Mario called to us in perfect English.

"Is it okay to bring my dog inside" I asked. "It will be very cold for him to be left in the car." I thought I saw Mario hesitate, before he beckoned us all inside.

The little house was very quaint, with thick insulating walls and old heavy furniture. The lighting was low and the big open fire gave a lovely warm glow. Next to the fire sat an old lady wearing a heavy shawl and with a knitted blanket over her legs. She was rocking gently in her chair and seemed to be asleep. At that moment, Anna appeared from the kitchen.

"This is my grandmother," she said quietly. The old lady opened her eyes and her wrinkled face broke into a smile. She bowed her head and raised her hand, giving us a weak wave in greeting.

The smells coming from the kitchen tempted us to investigate: it smelt fishy!

"I am cooking for you Bacalhau à Brás" said Anna, looking at us a little worriedly for our reaction.

"I hope you both like the Portuguese cod? It's called bacalhau". I handed her a bottle of good Portuguese red wine, which I had bought in the local shop on the way, before replying. "Oh yes, I love it. I'm sure Grace will like it too, but it will be a first for her." Grace followed me into the kitchen and Anna explained to her the method that the Portuguese have utilized to store and cook cod.

"During the 15th century, the Portuguese became pioneers for building large ships for cod fishing, they sailed far away to Greenland and Newfoundland for their catch." Anna poured us both a glass of fruity smelling red wine, before continuing. "Portugal has always produced salt, so the two became interlinked. In the early years, salting and drying the cod was the best way to keep it fresh without refrigeration; it was a cheap way to feed our people, but as time went on, our palate has come to love the flavour and texture of salted cod."

"I have to say," I broke in, "that when my very English palate first tentatively tried bacalhau, I didn't like it. My argument was why take a delicious piece of fresh cod, dip it in salt and dry it out, then re-constitute it by soaking it in fresh water before you eat it? Of course I could understand that before refrigeration, it made perfect sense: but now?"

Anna shrugged her shoulders. "It's a Portuguese tradition; did you know there are 365 recipes for cooking bacalhau?" I didn't; yet even with my biased views, I had come to really enjoy bacalhau. My favourite was barbecued, but bacalhau à brás is delicious, made by shredding the fish and mixing it with thinly cut fried chips, then stirring in scrambled eggs, olives and onion, before sprinkling plenty of parsley over the top. I was looking forward to enjoying my meal in this very good company. The wine that had been warming by the fire was very palatable too!

On another occasion earlier in the year, Steve and I were invited to a feast that was being laid on to celebrate the engagement of a young couple in our local village. The family lived in a big house on the edge of the village and we were looking forward to meeting new people and enjoying some Portuguese cuisine. I must admit that I also loved the chance to nose into other people's houses, so imagine my disappointment when we were led into a large underground room called an adega.

It was like a big cellar but on the ground floor, opening out onto the street. The electric lights had no shades on them, giving a harsh light, the walls were roughly rendered and the floor was concrete. Wine barrels covered a lot of the floor space, along with vats of olive oil and various other homemade alcohols. A pile of engagement presents lay in one corner, and we added our present to it. We had bought a beautifully embroidered tray cloth from our local seamstress; she assured me that they would love it although I thought it a little old fashioned.

There was a large trestle table covered by a brightly coloured plastic tablecloth, and as we arrived, the family were already bringing out plate after plate of scrumptious looking food. In the centre of the table was a huge brown intricately patterned ceramic pot of chanfana, which is braised goat in red wine; the carcass had been chopped up on the bone and cooked long and slow in a bread oven with lots of garlic and bay leaves. The bread that was on the table looked homemade and very crusty, perfect for mopping up juices.

The first time we had bought meat for a chanfana from our local butcher, we had been a bit taken aback when he had slung a large section of goat onto his chopping board and, raising his cleaver, chopped the carcass into small pieces, which he mixed together in a large bowl. Using this method, every customer was sold some pieces of lean meat along with more fatty rib meat, which all helped to make a really good stock. It's a very popular dish in this area of Portugal, where a lot of goats are kept.

Also on the engagement party table, were bowls full of yellow waxy boiled potatoes, liberally splashed with olive oil, and of course plenty of cabbage! Champagne glasses were filled, and we all raised our glasses to the health and happiness of the young couple.

Once the chanfana was just a pile of bones, desserts were brought out. Two large Pudims were placed in the centre of the table. There are many egg heavy desserts in Portugal as keeping chickens is part of their heritage, especially in the mountains. Pudim de ovos is no exception; made with eggs, sugar, milk and orange or lemon zest, then coated in a rich caramel sauce, it's very yummy! There were plates of rich cheesy queijadas, which are little tarts filled with ricotta and goats cheese, so nice with a glass of port!

The bride's father brought out an accordion, and the dancing started. Firstly the young couple danced a typical Portuguese folk dance together, before others joined in until the whole street was alive with dancing. We didn't know the steps, but there were plenty of willing teachers, and soon we were joining in with our arms held above our heads. We danced on into the dying embers of a magical day. I still wish that I had been able to have a peek at the interior of their rather stylish house though.

CHAPTER 9

A HORSE IN THE WORKSHOP

Craig arrived back from Morocco as brown as a berry...although I'm not sure where that phrase originated from! He seemed older and more mature as he told me of his experiences. One of the things that tickled him was that very young barefoot children were running around selling cigarettes singly, from a grimy screwed up cigarette packet. He thought it was a great idea as even he, on his meagre pocket money, could afford to smoke a cigarette. I was not so happy; but he was a teenager and of course he wanted to experiment.

Christmas was approaching, Steve was tired and miserable working in England, he desperately wanted to come home for Christmas, but it was a good time for taxi drivers, which was the job he was doing. A friend of his had his own taxicab and Steve still had his taxi licence, so it was easy for him to jump on a plane in Portugal, and start work the next day in Brighton. At this time of year, there were endless Christmas parties, where people needed a taxi; and of course, New Year's Eve was the busiest night of the year for taxi drivers. We considered ourselves lucky; we wouldn't have been able to finance our projects without this extra income. His friend had a spare room too, so Steve didn't even have to pay rent; it was a good safety net and we were grateful. He would work as many hours as possible all over Christmas and New Year, then arrive back home exhausted but hopefully with a pocket full of cash.

Mella phoned to tell me that she had finally finished with Bruce, and that she had a new boyfriend. It had all been very dramatic: Bruce had called at her home night after night, begging her to take him back, and threatening to kill himself. Then one night he lay down in the middle of the road outside her home and refused to move. Cars were swerving around him; the situation was out of control, so she phoned the police. They arrived and took him into custody but released him the next morning telling him to stay away from Mella. About a month later, he turned up at her door once again. It was answered by a very tall, well-built young man with twinkly green eyes. Bruce never bothered Mella again! That man eventually became the father of her two daughters, and his name is Simon.

Craig and I had been invited to my dear friend Denny's home, for Christmas dinner. It was an open house type of affair, we all chipped in with food and all helped to cook and serve. The saying 'too many cooks spoil the broth' took on a new meaning as half a dozen of us, all well inebriated with cocktails, danced around the kitchen to the music from The Sound of Music film, which was playing on the TV at full volume. Craig, and Denny's two sons Jay and Mo, stayed well out of our way!

For New Year, Craig and I walked along to Francisco's house where a huge bonfire was already burning. Most of the villagers were there, and a full-size hog was sizzling over the biggest barbecue I had ever seen. Some people had musical instruments and started playing Portuguese folk songs. A few were dancing, but most just stood around the fire, cupping glasses of wine. Francisco was singing and playing harmonica; he had a beautiful lyrical melodious voice, which I often heard drifting up from the fields while he was working. I loved to hear him singing or whistling while he planted his corn crop. It always gave me a feeling of quiet tranquillity.

At midnight came the fireworks; this is still a traditional Portuguese village event, and most villages have someone who makes fireworks. Bamboo poles of about six feet in height are gathered and cardboard tubes are filled with gunpowder and wrapped tightly in old sheets, then taped up well. The fireworks are not pretty at all; no bright sparkly colours lighting up the sky—it is all about the noise. The explosion is deafening, hopefully high up in the sky, although the fireworks seem to be a little erratic in direction! The men blast fireworks constantly into the ebony sky for about ten minutes, then it's all over; the night sky clears, and my poor battered eardrums can again hear the crackle of the fire and joyous people hugging, kissing, and making their New Year resolutions.

Two days later Steve was home. He had worked the night shift and gone straight to the airport to catch the first plane home. He was in Coimbra by 10 am waiting for me to pick him up. I had been up early, feeding and mucking out the horses before I left for the station. I drove as fast as I dared; I didn't want to get stopped by the police for speeding, but I just couldn't wait to see him again.

It was so lovely to have him home again; I had missed him so much. We spent a couple of days just enjoying being back together again and planning our next projects.

Steve was a carpenter by trade, he wanted to start making windows for the cottage, but he didn't have a workshop. He complained that every time he tried to build himself a workshop...I put a horse in it! I had to admit, there was some truth in his grievance. Before the horses moved to our home, he had done up an old stone shed to use as a workshop, but that now housed a horse. He had just started building a workshop tacked on to the end of our new stable block, but Duke, who was still stabled in the cottage, would need to move out, and Steve's new workshop was the perfect size!

Our local wood yard offered a solution. Chico, who owned it, was a charming man, small in stature, and with the ubiquitous burly moustache that decorated his upper lip like a long lost broom. He always had a ready smile and a genuine friendliness that made visiting him a pleasure. He had been let down on an order of windows and doors; they were all propped up in a corner of his workspace. Most of them were pretty much the size that we wanted. They were all double glazed and good hard wood. As our cottage was just a shell, it would be easy for Steve to custom fit the windows and doors by using either thicker or thinner frames where necessary. Chico said that Steve was welcome to use his machines and workspace to do any alterations, so a deal was struck and we now had windows and doors: the cottage was beginning to really take shape.

Alfonso was the local electrician and plumber. He was well along the road in years, and had cultivated a rotund belly on the way. I couldn't imagine him climbing a ladder, let alone having to crawl around in lofts or under sinks, yet he did! He had a big jowly face and thin wispy grey hair. He was the only electrician in the area, so the wait was long for his services. He expected Steve to do all the heavy work like digging down two metres outside the cottage for the earth rod to be installed, chasing out the walls, and digging trenches for the plumbing. Steve always said that he didn't mind digging, he liked the methodical process of the spade excavating the earth; he could let his mind wander to other things. In fact, he said that he had some of his best ideas while either digging or showering…not at the same time!

Our four crumbling stone walls were beginning to look like a pretty, cosy little cottage. We installed a small basic kitchen area, and a nice bathroom downstairs, which opened onto an open plan lounge area with a wood burning stove for the cooler months. Upstairs was a large mezzanine bedroom, overlooking the river and with views spanning the whole valley.

As soon as we had a website up and running, showing the cottage as accommodation, our bookings escalated. We were booked solid for the two months of summer; most of them were families needing two bedrooms, which meant the lovely spacious mezzanine bedroom had to be split into two, but needs must.

We were so excited that our dream was finally becoming a reality; our horses were fit and ready to work, and so were we. We felt ready to take on the world!

One day while shopping in the local supermarket, Steve felt a tap on his shoulder and looking round, he was confronted by an elderly Portuguese couple that he didn't recognise. They told him that they now lived in Lisbon but still owned the piece of forest and two small terraces next to our farm. Steve's ears pricked up…we had often wondered who owned this piece of land, it was very neglected and none of our neighbours had any contact address for the owners, but we had often thought that it was just about the right size for a horse-riding arena.

The couple didn't want much money for it; they just wanted to be rid of the responsibility for keeping it cleared. A deal was struck, and we hired a neighbour who was in the logging industry to come in and clear the land for us. It was mainly eucalyptus trees, a few pines, and an old rotting stump of the biggest cork oak tree I had ever seen. Cork oak trees are harvested every 10 years, their thick spongy cork skin being carefully removed by experts trained in the art. It is done by hand, using a knife and an axe. A 'year' number is then sprayed onto the stripped bark so that it is easy to see when the tree next needs to be harvested. It is slow and meticulous work and it is paramount that the tree is not damaged and is able to regenerate, but this poor old stump would not be regenerating any time soon.

Francisco had come along to 'help' with the clearing of the land, and when the old root of the cork oak was uncovered, his interest was piqued. He told us he would get his son-in-law to dig it up and take it away free of charge. Later we discovered it in his garden at the exact spot where he held his yearly New Year's Eve parties. It would make the biggest bonfire ever. Francisco told us that the old tree had stood proudly at the side of the road for centuries; but when the council decided to straighten the dirt road and lay tarmac, the poor old tree had been in the way and was felled.

Thankfully cork oak trees are now protected and it is illegal to cut them without permission. He also told us that five of the cork oaks standing on our land were suckers from that ancient tree, which was really nice to know. Cork oak trees are evergreen, the bright green, new leaves push off the old dull green/brown leaves, so the tree never stands bare like other species of oak. In autumn, their acorns are enjoyed by wild boar and we hear them snuffling for them at night. Jays hoard them for wintertime as do the cutest little chocolate brown squirrels that look exactly the same as red squirrels except for their colour.

Our first guests of the year arrived at Easter time. They were a Scottish family with a ten-year-old daughter. Mum and daughter, Chris and Sandy, were both keen riders, while dad, Robin, was a photographer. He had brought all his equipment with him, including his tripod. He loved to sit by the river early in the morning, before we were awake, and photograph wildlife at dawn. He was rewarded with some amazing shots of kingfishers diving for their breakfast, and a booted eagle soaring high; he saw a mongoose running along the river bank, but sadly he didn't manage to capture the elusive otters.

The arena was well under way, the land had been flattened out and our first truck load of wood chip, which was what we had decided to lay as a surface, was due. Our guests were self-catering which gave Steve time to supervise the trucks that were arriving daily with wood chip. The pile was enormous, and Robin was very keen to help spread it. He set up his camera on a tripod and filmed the whole procedure; there was no stopping him, he was out there with his shovel even before Steve.

Chris and Sandy were both good riders, Sandy was only ten years old, but very confident. She was riding Comet for his first full week of work. Comet had grown into a good-looking pony; he looked just like a Lusitano that had shrunk in the wash! He was a cheeky, affectionate pony; he had been my first-born foal, and I was very proud of him. He really seemed to like being ridden, working like a grown up with the other horses. Sandy loved him, she was always drawing cartoon pictures of him; she called him DotCom.

Chris rode Guv, who was his normal gentlemanly self, and I took the chance to ride my little 'sports car' Smartie, who was so popular with guests that I rarely got the chance to enjoy him. We had the most delightful fortnight with this family; I cannot put into words the joy of riding a spirited little 'sports car' horse through the woods and mountains in the spring sunshine. The sunlight sent arrows through the branches of the trees, touching the young green buds and tempting them to gradually unfold. It was easy to pick out the oak trees with their new bright green foliage, among the duller coloured pine and eucalyptus trees. There were still a few late blossoming Mimosa trees with their bright yellow flowers smelling of marzipan to brighten up all the greenery.

Underneath the forest canopy are multitudes of spring flowering shrubs including gorse, heather, broom, and a pretty little rock rose with blooms that are mostly white with yellow centres, but every so often, if you are lucky, you can find patches of a rarer bright pink variety. They are in the Cistus family, as is its big brother which is the most prolific flowering shrub colouring the hedgerows during April. This larger shrub grows to about two metres in height and has a strong perfume that is exuded through its oily leaves. The flowers are large and papery white with a maroon spot at the base of each petal and a bright yellow core. They are very delicate and about the size of a fried egg, hence, with their bright yellow core, we call them fried egg plants!

As we rode, we competed with each other to see who could spot all the different shades of green. There were so many; just when we thought we had covered them all, we would come across a different variety of green moss, crawling up an olive tree, or a new plant that had popped its little head up overnight; the list was endless. Puffball mushrooms littered the tracks, and every so often a horse would accidentally kick one, releasing thousands of orange spores into the air and up their nostrils, making them breathe out in a loud purring sound.

During the afternoons Robin, Chris and Sandy helped us spread the mountains of woodchip around the arena. It was hard work, yet Robin's camera made it all look easy. He had it set on a time lapse mode, making us look as if we were all zooming across the area with our wheelbarrows and spades. Talk about being on speed! On film, the job was done in 30 minutes, instead of more like 15 hours.

To say thank you to our helpers, we cooked a big barbecue for them on their last day's holiday. They had been here for two weeks, and had chosen to take our self catering option. When the family had first arrived they had bought a five kilo sack of pasta from the local shop. The running joke of the holiday was someone saying, "What's for dinner tonight, Mum?" and Mum would reply, "Pasta surprise." I never did find out if they were joking or not, but they certainly enjoyed the barbecue that we laid on for them. They booked to come back in the summer holidays but next time they all agreed to take the full board option...as long as there was no pasta on the menu!

The busy weeks of summer flew by, our new riding arena was a great success; we had come to the conclusion that most children didn't really want long rides, preferring to mix shorter hacks with riding in the arena. The horses and I were quite happy with this too, as long summer rides in the heat were taxing for them and me. A shorter morning ride, while the temperatures were still cool, then relaxing after lunch by the river, was a much more agreeable way of spending the hot summer days. Then during the long summer evenings, we had some fun in the arena. Parents were generally very happy to click their cameras as their child performed a simple dressage test that we had been practising all week, or jumped a small course of jumps. Duke excelled in the arena, he had been well trained in dressage and he loved to jump.

Inês, who had been my very first student, when we originally arrived here, was now 17 years old. She was about to attend a three-year course in horse management at a famous stud farm called Coudelaria de Alter do Chão which is in the Alentejo region of Portugal. It would mean her leaving home and living in at the stud farm, but if she worked hard she should, after three years, become a professional riding instructor, able to work in any realm of the horse world. She was excited, yet sad to be leaving her beloved Duke. She had become very attached to him over the past two years, but the stud had many fine horses and I was sure she would soon find a favourite.

A few weeks after Inês had left, I had a very tearful phone call from her; she was not getting on well with the course, the teaching was very strict and disciplinary, and the horses were all bad tempered, she had already fallen twice and she was losing confidence in her riding skills. Most of the students had taken their own horse with them on the course, so they didn't have to use the riding school horses. I knew what was coming next....

Please, would I sell Duke; please, please...her father was willing to pay. I felt I was being pushed into a corner, when suddenly I had an idea. The bookings for riding holidays were slowing down as October approached. "How about if I let you take him on loan until next Easter?" I urged. This would suit me because I would not have pay for his keep through the winter, and hopefully by next spring, Inês would be more confident and settled, and Duke could return here to us. I really didn't want to sell him.

We travelled down to Coudelaria de Alter do Chão with Duke. I wanted to make sure everything was in order and he would be well cared for. The stud really was a spectacular place, breeding top class Lusitano horses. If you ever travel to Portugal and you love horses, which you probably do if you are reading this book, you should try to visit; especially in spring when all the foals are born, it really is quite magical. The stud farm is open to the public.

CHAPTER 10

MY BROKEN LEG

We had a hay delivery planned and were expecting 250 bales of hay which all had to be stored in our barn. The hay truck backed down the drive and the sweet smell of good hay drifted into the autumn air. Our hay was stacked on wooden pallets in our barn to keep it away from the floor and to allow air circulation. We were about halfway through stacking, when I jumped down from the stack onto a pallet and my foot somehow slid through a hole and twisted. I fell heavily and heard the snap of bone.

Antonio, our hay man, jumped down from his truck where he had been throwing down the hay bales, looking very concerned. Steve also joined us.

"Are you ok?" Steve asked as he gently went to touch my leg.

"No, it's broken; I heard the snap."

"Oh shit, we will have to go to hospital and get it x-rayed."

"Just get me to the car and I will sit and wait for you to finish unloading." I said, with more confidence than I felt. Antonio and Steve both helped me to the car, which was parked close by; Steve went to fetch some pillows and tried to make me as comfortable as possible, then went back to finish the hay delivery. There is something very satisfying about a barn full of hay, and usually it gave me a nice, fulfilled feeling, but not this time as I lay helplessly on the back seat of the car, gritting my teeth in agony.

The x-ray at the hospital confirmed my prognosis, and I was put in plaster of paris right up to my knee. I was told not to do anything for six weeks but there was a problem with this. We had riding holiday bookings for the next four weeks and the first group were due tomorrow. We were expecting three ladies, two were friends and the other was a single lady travelling alone. All three were good riders and would be sharing the cottage. How were we going to cope?

Steve shrugged his shoulders.

"I will have to do the rides, I know the tracks from dirt biking and I helped you plan the routes, it will be a doddle."

"But Steve, you can hardly ride," I cried in dismay. I knew he was just putting on a brave face and that he was as demoralized as me. I had given him a few riding lessons in England and it had always been the plan that he should learn to ride properly, but there was never time, we were always so busy. There was an English girl called Alex, who lived locally and had ridden with me many times and therefore knew a few of my routes; I contacted her and told her the sorry story. She was happy to help, in fact she said she would really look forward to the challenge but she had never done the longer rides or the two picnic rides that we offered our guests.

Steve drove to the airport to pick up our guests; he couldn't find the words to tell them, so he just blandly chatted about other things. When he drove down our drive and I hobbled out to meet them on my crutches, the girls all looked perplexed. I introduced myself and told them the story of my untimely accident.

"So, who will be leading the rides?" one of the girls asked. I looked nervously at Steve who replied confidently.

"I will."

"Can you ride?" she asked, narrowing her eyes, her mouth twitching into a little smile.

"A bit" Steve answered truthfully.

"Great...we are going to have some fun this week," she squealed, giving her friend a high five.

The next morning, they all set out on their first ride. Jodie and Louise had been friends for years and rode regularly together; they were riding Apollo and Smartie. Becca who had booked independently, and had told me she loved Welsh cobs, was to ride Roxy. I had warned her that he could be a bit of a control freak and preferred to jog rather than walk, especially if there was a canter coming up, but she didn't seem fazed.

The three girls seemed to get on well even though they had only met yesterday. I had gone over the routes with Steve, telling him which paths were good for a trot and which paths were good for a canter, and after breakfast, they all set off on their first ride. I was left at home twiddling my thumbs!

I donned a black bin liner to cover my plaster of paris, tying it tightly above my knee. I then slowly but surely, mucked out three of the stables into the two wheelbarrows that we owned. I couldn't push them down to the muck heap which was about 30 metres away down a narrow stony path, so I just left them piled high and waited for someone else to come along to empty them for me. I hoped that maybe Francisco or one of my other neighbours would pass by and be happy to take the horse muck down onto their land.

My mind kept wandering: how was Steve getting on? Had he fallen off yet? He was riding Guv, who was the safest, kindest horse I had ever owned, but although Steve (and Guv) knew all of the routes, he was not experienced at riding out in the mountains on horseback; give him a motor bike and he was fine! His only experience of horse riding had been a few lessons in a riding school many years before.

It wasn't long before a car pulled up at the top of our drive and a couple walked down smiling. I had only met them once or twice briefly, but they had heard of my dilemma and had come to see if I needed any help. I was so grateful. Tommy and June had only moved to Portugal recently; they were doing up an old barn, and said they were glad of the distraction. They had been repairing walls and rendering for days, and June said her hands were raw from cement! They emptied the wheelbarrows for me and helped to finish off the remaining stables, then said they were going shopping and were happy to pick up anything I needed. That would be a great help as it would save Steve having to shop later, so I gave them a shopping list.

After they had left, I hobbled into the house on my crutches; I still wasn't very confident at going up and down stairs, so I would turn around and tackle the stairs on my bottom. Our kitchen was still upstairs in the main lounge, so once upstairs, I pulled a chair over to the sink and could just about reach to wash and dry all the breakfast things. I was watching the clock ticking by; straining to listen for the sound of hooves on tarmac. When at last I heard them, I almost slid down the stairs on my bottom, and was out in the yard anxiously waiting for them to dismount. They were all in a jovial mood; they must have had a good time…for all my worrying.

"How did it go?" I asked apprehensively

"Fine, once we taught Steve how to gallop," Jodie laughed, as she hosed down a sweaty Apollo.

"He was trying to sit in the saddle when we galloped, and he kept losing his stirrups," she continued. "Once we shouted to him to stand up in the stirrups and lean forward, there was no stopping him!" joined in Becca, as she reached for the hose to wash off a very sweaty Roxy who had already started to grow his Welsh winter coat.

I noticed that after Steve had hosed down Guv, he made his way rather stiffly into the house. I hobbled after him and he told me that his derriere was very sore. On closer inspection, I could see that he had broken the skin on both cheeks; it was not looking good. I phoned Alex and asked her if she could possibly take the girls out riding on the following day. Luckily, she agreed. I asked the girls if they would be happy to go for a shorter hack in the morning, and we would put up some jumps and have a little competition in the afternoon. They 'jumped' at the chance; so at least poor Steve could have a day off to heal his injuries.

The next morning, I once more waited anxiously for the four women to return from their ride, but again I needn't have worried, they had all enjoyed themselves and were looking forward to the big jumping finale that was to take place that afternoon.

Roxy, Comet and Smartie were all good jumpers, so the three girls practised over the jumps that Steve had erected in the school, swapping horses and having fun. I was commandeered as photographer. All three girls wanted me to take photos on their own cameras, so I was kept busy. After a while Steve announced that he would raise the height of one of the jumps after each round. If your horse knocked down a pole, you were disqualified. The winner would be the pair who jumped the highest. I had a feeling that Roxy and Becca would win, and I was right; Roxy had always been a good careful jumper. One of the areas where I used to ride him in England had solid wooden picnic tables with attached benches, set in the woodland; Roxy and I would jump them just for fun, as long as there were no picnickers of course!

My friend Sophie came to visit me. She was not confident enough to help take out the rides, but she had promised to help out on the picnic rides. David, her boyfriend had offered to lend her his Land Rover which would manage the tracks much easier than a car. Sophie said she would bring a tasty picnic, and I was really looking forward to having a day out, I was getting fed up with being left at home alone every day!

Next morning, I covered Steve's bottom with plasters to try to protect his injured skin, and they all set off on the horses for the picnic location. Sophie and I set off about an hour later in the Land Rover; Steve had already packed it with table and chairs before he had left, so we only had to pack the picnic. Sophie had made a delicious looking smoked salmon quiche and had bought a bag of salad to accompany. She had stopped at the local bakery and bought fresh rolls and had also brought some goat's cheese from her own larder, and a really squishy ripe sheep's cheese. The smells emanating from Sophie's picnic hamper made my mouth water: this was the best day I'd had since before my accident.

We were heading for the gorgeous gorge, as we called it. This was my favourite picnic ride because we could swim (not me this time!) in the cool deep pool of the gorge, before tucking into our feast. The last time we had visited the gorge, Apollo had been traumatised by a rave party in full swing, but this time all was quiet and he didn't seem to remember his trauma. The horses loved this spot because we made them a paddock out of electric string that had no electricity running through it. We just relied on the fact that they could gorge on the fresh green grass growing along the river's edge, and wouldn't notice the lack of electric current! Little frogs jumped out of the way as the horses' big hooves sunk into the muddy bank, and they all drank their fill of the cool clear water.

The following day was the horses' and Steve's bottom's day off! Our guests had decided to take the train into the city of Coimbra. It was an hour's scenic journey on an old train that chugged through the valleys and little villages, only stopping twice at bigger towns on the way. The girls told us later of their adventures.

They took a boat ride on the river Mondego, with the city towering over them. Coimbra, which dates back to Roman times, was built on a steep hill, so all of the streets lead upwards or downwards. The girls found some interesting old shops in the lanes area to buy souvenirs, and they discovered a busy authentic restaurant for lunch. They also found the oldest medieval house that dates back to the fifteenth century. In the afternoon, they climbed the cobbled hills and hundreds of steps that led to the top of the city, where the university sits. They all scowled when later I told them that there was a glass lift that went from the bottom to the top of the City!

Coimbra university dates back to 1537, and has been in constant use ever since. The students make Coimbra a very lively city, and they still adhere to old traditions like wearing long black robes for many of the functions and festivities, including Queima das Fitas. During this tradition, the students parade around the streets to celebrate their graduations, accepting many free tipples from bar owners on their journey to a park, where a party goes on for a week, with a full programme of singers, dancers, and DJs to liven up the nights. Oh, to be a student again!

Our guests paid a visit to the oldest library in Portugal, constructed in 1728 in the Baroque style. They all agreed that the building was very beautiful with many ancient books, but you could only visit with a tour guide and they were not allowed to take photos, which they were all a bit peeved about.

The next morning, my friend Alex took them riding again, and in the afternoon we had a dressage session in the riding arena. Steve's bottom was healing nicely which was lucky because on the last day of the girls' holiday, we had planned the longest ride of the week, with a picnic on top of the world!

Sophie had again prepared us a delicious lunch and was driving the Land Rover to the picnic location. This mountain location meant that we would have to do a lot of off-road driving, which would be fun as long as we didn't get stuck or lost! We arrived in plenty of time to set up the picnic, and we both had our cameras ready to capture the horses and riders galloping towards us. We were on a ridge track which ran along the top of the mountain at a height of just under 1000 metres.

The horses knew this gallop well, and all loved to race to the picnic spot. I could see Roxy in the distance, leaping up in the air in excitement, Becca controlling him well. How I wished it was me riding him; me feeling the exhilaration of galloping along a mountain top, instead of standing here on crutches. The riders all released their reins and they were off at a fast gallop. Roxy always started in the lead but with his shorter hairy legs, he was soon overtaken by Guv the Thoroughbred, and Smartie the Arab, both much faster breeds than a Welsh Cob. But he never gave in, and as Guv and Smartie slowed down to a trot as they approached us, Roxy saw his chance, and barged past them into the lead again, as if to say 'I won!'

The picnic was enjoyed by all; spicy fried chicken with a home-made potato salad, followed by a sticky, sweet, yummy baklava that Sophie had made. She had also bought a bottle of Vinho Verde which is a young Portuguese white wine with a little bit of fizz, which really hit the spot! The views at this height were spectacular, you could literally see for miles. There was a higher mountain to one side of us, and on the other side we looked down on tiny white villages that looked like dolls' houses. The breeze that was blowing up through the heather clad hillside had a sweet tang of wild flowers and herbs.

We were above the tree line and as we all stood marvelling at the vista, an eagle took off from a branch right below us, its mighty wings outstretched, lazily scanning the valley below. We watched its head twitch and saw its fierce eyes lock onto a movement below, then, in a split second the bird dived down onto some unsuspecting small mammal, and with an easy flap of its powerful wings it soared upwards and landed on a branch to devour its meal.

As we stood looking into the distance, we saw storm clouds rapidly forming and advancing in our direction. The forecast had been for rain, so at the last minute Sophie had bundled the horse's rugs into the car. Now everyone ran to collect them, and as the first raindrops fell, they just managed to cover the horses in time, before making a dash for the car. I had already hobbled back to the car, and settled myself into the front seat, but we were all a little bit damp, and as we huddled into the car along with sweaty saddles, it steamed up within minutes. For the next half hour, we girls told horsey stories and polished off the wine, while Steve sat watching the skyline, looking bored. Once the storm had moved away, a rather soggy group of horses and riders made their way home. Steve had made it through the first week, and was now an experienced horse rider.... the next three weeks would be no problem!

A very kind neighbour had offered to come in on Saturdays to change the bedding and clean the cottage, which was a great help as I was still pretty useless, and Steve needed to go shopping and prepare some meals, so by Saturday afternoon we were ready to receive the next five guests. They were a split family of two young girls, aged 12 and 14 years, the girls' parents, and also the mother's new lover!

The sleeping arrangements were that the girls would be sharing a bedroom in our house with their father, while their mother, Lucy and lover Russsell (who actually looked just like a young Russell Crowe) stayed in the cottage. The two girls Jessie and Sara were horse mad, and both good riders, as was their mother. Russell was going to accompany them on foot; he was very athletic! Father was to stay at home. Both of the girls had a crush on Russell and were too young to hide it. They hung on his every word, whilst their poor father faded into the background. I felt so sorry for him, but it was none of my business.

On the first two mornings Steve led the ride on his favourite horse Guv, and everything went well. Russell followed behind on foot with earphones firmly affixed, often jogging to keep up. My friend Alex had enjoyed her time as ride leader the week before, and had agreed to lead the picnic ride to the gorgeous gorge on the third day as Steve was again having problems with his posterior. She knew most of the tracks but there were some that she didn't know, so the day before, Steve took her on his motorbike around the tracks until she felt confident that she wouldn't get lost.

Next morning, they all set out for the picnic ride. Alex was riding Roxy and Lucy was riding Guv, the young girls were riding Smartie and Comet, with Russell bringing up the rear on foot, complete with headphones as usual. No one really knew what happened but for no apparent reason, Comet became agitated and bucked his young rider off, he then barged riderless and still bucking, past Smartie causing his young rider to fall to the ground also! Their mother was shouting hysterically although both girls were up and on their feet without injury.

They managed to catch their ponies and with the help of Russell they both re-mounted giggling. The girls thought the whole incident had been funny, but their mother Lucy was still shouting at poor Alex, who thankfully managed to keep control of the situation, and the group all arrived safely at the picnic spot.

Comet was usually a good natured pony, and as we sat discussing the incident over a glass of wine at the gorge, while the girls splashed in the river with Russell, we came to the conclusion that he must have been stung by a hornet or horse fly in a rather sensitive area! This sort of thing did happen occasionally, horse fly attacks were a constant threat in the long hot summers, but it was just bad luck that it happened when Alex was in charge.

Our farrier Tom had become a good friend, and when he heard of our dilemma, he offered to learn one of our picnic rides to help us out, so on the guest's day off, Steve and Tom set out in his jeep up the steep rocky tracks. It had taken me ages to learn this tricky ride, yet Tom learnt it in one afternoon. He said he felt confident that he could lead the ride on the following day. He was an experienced rider and Guv would help him out as he knew the ride like the back of his hooves! Everyone enjoyed their last ride; we even managed to tire Russell, who asked if he could come home in the car with us.

The next week we had four Swedish people booked in. Three were good regular riders, but one lady called Annalie, could not ride at all. She had promised me beforehand that she would be taking an intensive riding course so that she could participate with her friends, but when she arrived she told us that she hadn't had the time to have any lessons at all. So, we had a non-rider on our hands; she obviously didn't realise the amount of skill needed to control a horse out in the mountains. Her friends were very understanding of the situation and told us that they were happy just to walk the horses for the first ride, and see how it went from there.

After a two hour walk, poor Annalie was completely numb and sore, so the next day she rested. She was a doctor, specialising in brain surgery, and told me that she had lots of work to catch up on. She was so engrossed in her work that she didn't miss her friends at all, but I felt that she should have some horse action seeing as she had paid for a riding holiday. I asked her if she would like me to give her some lessons on Smartie, and she readily agreed, so over the next few days, I hobbled into the arena and from the comfort of a chair, I gave her basic lessons in walk and trot.

In the meantime, Steve was really starting to enjoy his job. He was riding daily with the three other guests, one was a young man from the north of Sweden, he spoke with the typical lilt of the region; he reminded me of the Swedish chef from Sesame Street! When he first introduced himself, he told us,

"I'm into extreme sports" pitching each word from high to low. He was certainly a good rider, and so was his wife. Steve told me that they used to gallop holding hands on the wider tracks, the horses racing neck to neck. On the last day, Annalie joined them out on a quiet ride; she could now trot perfectly, and was really pleased with her new skill. She said she would try to keep up lessons in Sweden because her work was so engulfing that she really needed a hobby.

The final week of October was booked by two adult sisters, unfortunately it was a bit of a washout, with rain and storms all week long; the three intrepid explorers came back home each day muddy, drenched, and cold, but still with smiles on their faces.

CHAPTER 11

TOBY THE DOG

November was a time for sitting around the fire, recouping our energies and planning our next project. We were finally going to build a proper kitchen in our downstairs dirt floored room. Steve had already knocked a doorway through from the outside, and fitted glass doors to give as much light as possible, but the room still needed more light, so he planned to knock out a large window through stone and mud walls of more than one metre in thickness that had stood undisturbed for hundreds of years. The stones used to build the house were local round river boulders of different sizes, not nice square blocks, so it was impossible to know what he would come across once he made the first blow. It was an enormous undertaking and he was very nervous.

My plaster had just come off and my leg had healed well but was very weak, with no muscle left. I would be of no help in lifting huge boulders out of the wall, but my eldest son Paul was coming to visit for six weeks and Craig was also on hand to help at the weekends. The hole grew larger; it was incredible to see the size of some of the boulders that came out of the wall. In Portugal the sun still has some strength in November, and luckily it shone down on us for the whole time that the hole was open. At night we covered the hole with thick plastic, and put on an extra jumper! It was wonderful having Paul staying with us, he lifted all our spirits with his indomitable good humour and enthusiasm.

Mella and Simon were visiting for Christmas; we would all be together as a family for the first time in quite a few years. Sadly for one very important member of our family, it would be his last Christmas. Toby the dog was ailing; he was over 14 years old and having problems negotiating steps and stairs. Sometimes his back end would give out on him and he needed help to get up and down stairs. He looked old and tired, his muzzle was completely white. He had always been such a strong athletic dog that it was heartbreaking to watch his demise.

Paul and Mella had always had very strong feelings for Toby. Paul had been 13 years old, Mella had been 9 and Craig was just a baby when Toby arrived at our home as a 4-month-old puppy. He had been rescued by the R.S.P.C.A, suffering from neglect, abuse and malnutrition. The animal charity had done a wonderful job, nursing him back to health but he was still skinny and nervous and was crouching at the back of his cage, when my little girl spied him there. Mella and I often popped into the kennels to pet the dogs when we were passing, and had got to know the lady in charge of the kennels. She told us that black dogs were always the hardest to re-home, so she didn't hold out much hope for this poor little pup.

But Mella was squeezing my hand, and with eyes welling with tears, she begged me to let her have him. She kneeled down in front of his cage, and spoke gently to him. His tail flickered nervously on the floor, and still crouching low to the ground, he crawled forward, his eyes watching her all the time. She put her fingers through the bars and his little nose sniffed them tentatively. Tears welled in my eyes too and of course I gave in, and after having a home check by the rescue centre, Toby came home with us. He grew into a beautiful big black Labrador type of dog, and was loved by all of the family, but especially Paul and Mella; and they still loved him now.

Throughout his life, I had never allowed to call him a dog; they would always correct me. "Mum he is not a dog, he's a man". During their teenage years, they had concocted a passport and a driving licence for him; he even had his own bank account! But now he was a very old man and he sensed their grief as they sat stroking him. He seemed to make a big effort to be more active, Paul slept with him every night on a mattress in front of the fire, and Mella drew a beautiful picture of him, which we still have today.

We had a lovely Christmas, but only one week after my two elder children returned to England, Toby sadly passed away in his sleep. He will never be forgotten by any of us and he is buried in our garden under a tangerine tree which gives tasty juicy fruits each Christmas.

Our riding holidays were already booked up for Easter, and Inês was due to bring Duke back from the Alentejo. She was not happy and again begged me to sell him to her. It just happened that our lovely hay supplier Antonio phoned me to say that his friend had a horse for sale and he thought we may be interested. I arranged to meet him and together we went to visit his friend.

The horse was a real stunner; he was a dun colour with a long black mane and tail. I took him out for a short ride to try him out, and although he was not naughty in any way, he had no schooling and would need a lot of training, but he had a nice calm manner and very good looks. I liked him and the price that he had given Antonio would be affordable if I sold Duke to Inês, so imagine my shock as we started negotiating, to learn that the price had doubled!

Antonio was furious, he and his friend broke into a full-blown argument; they were talking so fast that I couldn't understand all that they were saying. After a few minutes, Antonio took my arm and we marched off together. He was fuming; I could almost see the steam coming from him.

"It's because you are a foreigner," he said when he had calmed down a bit.

"I will take you to see another horse that is for sale close by." And this was where I first saw Haraquiri.

Antonio took me to Mafalda's yard. I had met her some years before when she had let me ride her white Lusitano stallion called Calico. She had ridden him in exhibitions and shows all around Europe, he was highly trained and riding him had taken my breath away. They obviously had a great rapport together, and although I was the one riding him, he was listening to her. When she clicked her tongue to the beat of piaffe which is a high-class dressage move, Calico performed piaffe for me. I just sat there feeling as if I were on a cloud; he was so light in my hands.

Riding him had been an experience that I would never forget so I was very upset to learn that he had passed away. Calico had been given to Mafalda as a foal for her christening present. They had grown up together, she must have been devastated when he died, but he gave her one last gift…his son. She was training him now as we approached her yard; he was a dark grey Lusitano, but only four years old so he would eventually become white just like his father.

Mafalda took us to see the horse that she had for sale. He had spent most of his life as a professional show jumper, but she had bought him to train for dressage and had found him to be a natural. She said that he enjoyed learning and she was sure he would go far He was half Lusitano and half English Thoroughbred; he had beautiful kind expressive eyes, and his name was Haraquiri. At 1.70m he was much bigger than I was looking for and also much too expensive. I came home feeling disappointed, both horses had been lovely but both had been too expensive. Duke was proving to be a hard horse to replace, especially as I really didn't want to sell him. Maybe I should just be hard on Inês and insist that she brought Duke home to me.

I was still mulling over the problem a few weeks later, when I had a phone call from Mafalda. She had seemed so upbeat and positive when I had spoken to her two weeks ago, but appearances can be deceptive, and now as she poured her heart out to me over the phone, I realised that her life was a mess. She had just found out that she was pregnant and not by her husband. Consequently her marriage was breaking up and she had to sell Haraquiri. She said she knew I would look after him so she offered him at a price I could afford. Although I was sorry for Mafalda, my heart leapt; Haraquiri was a beautiful horse with the ability to teach me a lot as well as my guests. I phoned Inês and gave her the news. Of course, she was ecstatic, and so was I, I felt sure that Haraquiri would be a great horse for us.

Harry is a family name, Steve's dad was called Harry, and Steve and Craig both have Harry as a second name, so Haraquiri became Harrie. It suited him, and I was a little worried that his full name might cause people to be nervous of riding him…in English it translates as Hara-kiri; a form of ritual suicide and disembowelment practised by the Japanese Samurai!

It hadn't occurred to me that Harrie would not have been ridden outside of an arena very often. He was fine with the hustle and bustle of a show jumping event, and very trustworthy in traffic, but when faced with a small tree that had fallen across a track, he got himself into a tizz; he didn't understand that he was allowed to just step over it, he thought he had to jump it, so he did—almost landing on the back of the horse in front! We had our first guests of the year arriving in two weeks' time, so I was going to have to ride him regularly out into the forest, to reassure him that he would now be living an easier, less stressful life.

I feel that hacking out in the countryside is the most natural way to ride a horse. It is the closest to how they would behave in the wild. Just walking along shady mountain tracks, following the horse in front; occasionally trotting or cantering, and when the tracks were good enough, some exciting bursts of speed, which the horses seemed to enjoy as much as we humans!

Harrie settled in well, and was very popular with our guests. Within his first two seasons with us, he had as many mentions in our guest book as Guv and Smartie. I thought you may like to read a few of our guest comments so have added some below.

Julie and Pete.   *The human company was excellent (hosts and fellow guests alike). Many stories shared, the world put to rights several times, good food, music and the wine flowed. The supporting cast of Moppy, Bica, Misty BB and Robin and of course Bastard Bun added constant amusement. Add the stars of the show, Roxy, Harrie, Guv, Comet and especially "quick Smartie" and the prancing pony Apollo who danced the whole week! All the ingredients needed for a special week that will be long remembered.*

Sue and Roger.   *I'm an atheist, but this week I would almost believe there is a benevolent God! Everything has been perfect— horses, calm but forward going as promised, accommodation rustic but comfortable, and the setting in this valley and this area of Portugal generally, quite paradisiacal! And as for the company; the humour, and the food....very heaven. Thanks so much Steve and Sandra, I hope we will be back.*

Dagmar and Zara.   *This had been the perfect holiday for us: glorious weather, stunning scenery, cosy accommodation, heavenly food, wonderful animals (big kiss for Moppy) beautiful horses.*

(Big hugs for noble Guv and swift Smartie.) Swimming in the river especially on rides, and above all hosts to die for: warm, generous, with a great sense of humour and big hearts! Thank you Steve and Sandra for all you have done and for being who you are. We will be back!

John and Bridgid. *Thank you so much for letting us share your little corner of Paradise for a week. It was a really special holiday and we could not have hoped for more. It felt like we had gone to stay with friends for a week, I am definitely more confident with horses and looking forward to improving and coming back next summer.*

Dad Paul. *Well worth getting a sore bum for!*
Daughters Holly and Hatty. *This had been a great week yet again. All the horses were perfect. Thanks for letting us jump on Harrie and Comet. It was brilliant and a real confidence giver. Big hugs to Smartie Moppy Bica , Comet and Harrie.*
P.S. Can't wait for next year. Xxxxx

Roy and Piri Piri Sue. *Came as guests, left as friends! Hippy horsewoman and surfer dude, cheers for a great holiday.*
P.S. Don't eat the babies!! (this refers to baby ducklings that were born while they were here)

Phil-Jayne-Emma. *Phil: well planned rides and the best bog roll in the world=a perfect holiday. Love from the drunks next door!!*
P.S. Comet rules.
Jayne. *Roxy has found a place in my heart, I loved riding him; he was great fun, especially the 360 spins!*
Emma. *It was my dream to go on a riding holiday. This week outshone my wildest dreams, with my trusty mount Smartie, who I kissed often! Lovely hosts, and a menagerie of all creatures great and small. The food was not up to much...only joking Steve! Love hugs and kisses to you all, you will stay with me forever.*

Jodie and Gavin. *Food heavenly and you are marvellous hosts but most importantly, your horses are a real asset to you. Harrie is an angel, please only allow nice guests to ride him. Thanks for the surprise champagne picnic ride to celebrate our anniversary. Loved swimming in the river and please do not change too much!*

Nick and Nicky. *Thank you for a lovely week. Harrie was a perfect pleasure to ride and Guv a great confidence giver for Nick. Thanks also for accommodating Nick's gluten free diet with such inventive enthusiasm! We are both feeling relaxed and refreshed and glad that we met the Hollicks in the queue at Gatwick all those months ago and took their recommendation to come here.*

Claire. *I was very anxious about coming alone, but have had a brilliant time. I couldn't have anticipated better horses. Smartie was fantastic and has given me more confidence.*

Maria and Tony. *(both in their 60's) Your horses are a credit to you, last year I rode Guv, this year I rode Harrie; I have decided to call him "Pegasus" the flying horse. I felt extremely safe and confident with this wonderful friend. Tony is a nervous rider, but Guv as always looked after him, another fantastic friend. The meals were to die for and Bica and Moppy were always loving. Change nothing, it is Paradise. See you next year.*

Su and Jon. *And the plan is...we'll be back.*

Yvonne and Graeme. *From the moment the first trot turned into a flat out gallop, the huge grin never left my face. Harrie is a lovely ride and drop dead gorgeous too. Every woodland trail had its own unique atmosphere, and the wildlife, especially the black squirrel was a real bonus. Great company and food. Totally Magic!*

Gill and Colin. *Well here we are again, what a way to celebrate being 40! Riding Brill, Food fab, looking forward to coming back already! Colin loved his time on your motorbike Steve!* (Colin and Gill have been coming twice a year for more than 10 years, and are still great friends today.)

There are many, many more, I'm sure when I look back and read this visitors book in years to come, I will feel a warm glow in my heart. One of the above guests mentioned Bastard Bun, and I realised that I have forgotten to tell his tale so here goes.

An English family were moving back to England. This happens with a lot of ex-pats; their new life didn't turn out to be exactly what they expected. This family had bought an angora rabbit for their daughter, but she had lost interest in it and didn't want to take it back to England with her, so they asked me if I would take the rabbit. Begrudgingly I agreed, I had enough mucking out to do, but I do like small animals and had always had rabbits and guinea pigs as a child. Sadly, the rabbit was badly neglected; angoras need lots of care and grooming and I wouldn't think this poor little guy had ever been groomed in his life. He had a huge solid ball of hair under his chin and he could barely move his head, he also had clumps of matted fur under his belly, and his back end was absolutely filthy. I didn't know where to start clipping and cleaning him.

Our guest for that week was a Portuguese nurse, she was due to leave on the day that the rabbit arrived. She was so upset by his condition that she spent her last two hours with him on her lap, clipping him with her surgical scissors which luckily she had brought with her. The rabbit was very nervous and tried to move and jump away. I would have found it very scary to have to clip him so close to his skin with him making quick, jerky movements, but Maria just went to work with gentle tiny little clips while I tried to hang on to him and keep him as calm and still as possible. After two hours the lump of fur under his chin was off and he was almost bald under his tummy and around his bottom. He looked a mess, but he must have felt so much better.

We let him stretch his legs and run around on our veranda, which was a fairly safe area. He was really very sweet and inquisitive. He had a cage but it was quite small, so I started letting him run around in our lounge each day. I paid the price for my kindness; he left me lots of little brown balls all over the floor! What he needed was a nappy. I bought a pack of the smallest sized baby disposable nappies, and even found some designed for swimming which were more absorbent. The nappies were bright green with little froggie patterns on them; I put a pair onto bunny, he didn't seem to mind at all, and loved the freedom of hopping around our house.

The dogs more or less ignored him except for poor little Moppy, who he had taken a shine to: he chased her relentlessly, until he discovered the cats. Misty was languishing in a sunny spot on the carpet one day when bunny hopped right on top of her, green swimming nappy and all! It was love at first sight for him, but was not reciprocated by Misty; she was horrified and ran for her life all around the furniture with bunny in hot pursuit. He was having a great time, he was as agile as her and as she leapt up onto the computer keyboard, he followed, hot with desire! The telephone, pens and papers were scattered into the air as the pair ran over the computer desk, until eventually Misty was cornered and reacted as most cats would; she attacked him. He jumped up into the air in shock with blood dripping from his nose. Well, that will teach him a lesson, I thought as I returned him to his cage to recuperate.

But no: his memory was short and the next day, bright green nappy firmly in place, he ran around searching for his heart's desire. Misty took one look at him and fled; I ran to open the door for her to escape, she shot through my legs and I just managed to close the door before bunny bolted for his freedom. He was becoming a nightmare, but that was not all; he chomped through wires, jumped up onto the table and selected his favourite fruits from the fruit bowl, and he managed to find a way of kicking off his nappy, sprinkling his little balls of poo in every direction. He certainly earned his name...Bastard Bunny!

A lovely family had started to have riding lessons with me, the children loved to pet Bastard Bun (I didn't tell them his real name) and when I mentioned that I was looking for a new home for him, the mother pulled me to one side and said she was looking for a rabbit for her son. They already had a female rabbit which belonged to her daughter, and she had promised her son his own pet for his birthday. By now Bastard Bun's hair had grown through and he was a very handsome boy, but he would have to be castrated if he was to live with a female rabbit; I knew what a stud he was! We agreed to go halves on the castration and the operation went well. Within a week, Bastard Bun moved to his new home, and hopefully a new name!

CHAPTER 12

DOMINO

It had been a busy year for us, we had met some amazing people, some of whom would become good friends, but it wasn't always without mishap. One time, we had a group of four riders staying with us and had just enjoyed a lovely picnic ride. On the way home, Roger, the least experienced of the group, lost a stirrup while galloping; he lost his balance and agonisingly tried to uproot a big pine tree. The tree won: and the following day, Roger had the most immense and colourful bruises I had ever seen.

Ever a glutton for punishment, the couple returned the following year, and this time Roger managed to return home with the same colour skin as he arrived with. They returned later in the year on a house hunting expedition. Both were smitten with this green heart of Portugal, and I knew how they felt, but even I was surprised when they returned from a house viewing trip and announced that they had bought two properties!

Another very colourful guest was a lady from the Isle of Wight. She wanted a single room with her own bathroom. I explained that the only single room we had did not have a bathroom, and she would be sharing the bathroom with us. She seemed very dissatisfied with this and I didn't expect to hear any more from her. A few days later, she phoned again asking if she would have a double bed in her room, I assured her that she would have a double bed but would be sharing a bathroom. I explained that we were not a hotel but a rustic farm.

Felicity booked a holiday with us, but didn't book a flight home or give us a leaving date. We didn't envisage that this would be a problem, because our single room was not occupied much. Most people preferred to stay in our cottage or our double bedroom, so if she wanted to stay on for longer, that would be fine.

What I didn't realise until she arrived was that she had been internet dating a Portuguese man, and couldn't book a flight home because she didn't know how things were going to work out once they met in the flesh. Steve picked Felicity up from the airport, and had already formed a bad opinion of her by the time they arrived home. He said her main topic of conversation was how many rich boyfriends she'd had. She told him, and me as soon as she arrived, that she would only date men with flashy new cars; and as we helped her unload her two massive cases from our old Renault van, she casually mentioned that she trained in polo at the same yard as our British Royal family. I thought she had brought her worldly goods with her, but it turned out to be mainly shoes. High heeled sling back types in beautiful colours, but hardly suitable for farm life!

We had a lovely young couple riding and staying in our cottage, they had two days left of their holiday when Felicity arrived. Paul had proposed to Sarah down by our river, how romantic! We introduced them to a Bob Dylan song "Wild is the wind" and they adopted it as their special song. We were all sitting on the veranda sipping cold wine waiting for Felicity to join us for dinner, when the door flew open and this blur of white towelling robe stormed through. Without waiting for introductions, her first line was "Do you mind if I sit at the table with my face mask on?" Her face was bright blue, and she was totally unaware of our astonished faces.

As she told us her life story we realised that her glamorous life was tinged with a lot of sadness. Her mother had died when she was a child and she was brought up by her abusive father. She had been married three times and had two children. Her eldest son never visited her and her teenage daughter was out of control. Felicity said that she couldn't cope with her rebellious daughter, so she had just left her to her own devices. She did seem to know a lot of famous people, and name dropped constantly. How was she going to fit in on our rustic farm, and could we cope with her?

The next morning, Paul, Sarah and I were all mounted on our horses and waiting for Felicity to emerge. Duke was back with us, but that's another story! Felicity asked which horse she would be riding and when I pointed to Duke who was a very bright chestnut, she said "Oh no, not in burgundy jodhpurs", and disappeared back into her bedroom. After five minutes she finally emerged wearing a very tight top (she was a buxom lady) and white jodhpurs. I'm sure that as the week wore on, more and more male neighbours just happened to be strolling down the road as they heard the clip clop of our horses' hooves!

When Paul and Sarah returned home, Felicity asked if she could invite her internet boyfriend to dinner. He was from Porto and it would be their first meeting. We agreed to cook them a nice meal and then make ourselves scarce. I was peeping through a crack in the curtain as I heard his car come down our driveway. It was a bright red BMW open top sports car, and inside at the wheel was Marco; a very handsome, very young Portuguese man.

Now Felicity was at least 45 years old but the photo that she used on her internet page was of her much younger self. I would say Marco was about 25 years old and it was impossible not to notice the absolute shock on his face as Felicity skipped down our steps and ran to meet him in clothes that were way too tight for her more than voluptuous figure. There were some raised voices before he jumped back into his car and zoomed off and she stormed into her bedroom and slammed the door. We had been planning to eat scrambled egg on toast for our tea but it looked as if we would be eating gourmet food after all!

One morning Felicity arrived in the yard to ride, wearing a crop top with her belly hanging out over her jodhpurs. She had taken a liking to our Portuguese honey, and ate slice after slice of bread spread with thick butter and honey for her breakfast every morning. I could virtually see her getting fatter by the day!

"How do I look?" she asked, as she often did. Normally I replied "Fine", but on this morning I quipped, "That's a bit tight for you isn't it?" She flew back into her bedroom in a rage and came back out wearing a completely see-through blouse and a bright red bra. This would really please the neighbours, I thought.

Felicity's bedroom opened directly onto our lounge where our main phone and computer workstation was. One night Steve had forgotten to take a glass of water to bed with him so he got up in the night for a drink. He heard Felicity talking and assumed that she was using our phone. Next morning, he asked her if she had been on the phone and she denied it. He didn't trust her; phoning abroad was very expensive in those days, and we only phoned internationally when it was absolutely necessary. We had a setting on our phone to check all calls, and sure enough she had made five one-hour calls to England since she had been with us. Again she denied it, saying she was talking to Marco in Porto. But the telephone numbers had been recorded, and they all had the 0044 British code. She was lying to us, and finally she relented, saying that her teenage daughter was in big trouble and she needed to talk with her. We tried to reason with her that maybe she should be at home with her daughter, but she said she was still hoping that Marco would be in touch once he had calmed down. Our computer was on dial up at this time, so also expensive to use the internet, and when we checked our computer history, we found that she had been spending hours looking at properties in Portugal and France.

By now, Steve could not bear to be in the same room as her.

"Have you booked your ticket home?" he blurted out.

"No, I haven't," she snapped. "I have Marco's address, you can drop me off at his house in Porto, I'm sure if I just turn up on his doorstep, he will be pleased to see me."

I wasn't so sure, but Steve was adamant that she was leaving, and an hour later they set off for Porto. I was pleased to see her go; she was vain and rude and would trample people to get her own way, yet there was a sad vulnerability about her that I couldn't quite put my finger on.

Duke had been back with us for the summer; it had been a lovely surprise when Inês had phoned to ask if he could come home. She had a three-month summer vacation from her college, and although she could leave Duke at the college, she would prefer to bring him home so that she could continue to ride him. Her family only lived about 10 minutes from us, so it made perfect sense. We had to de-clutter our huge shed to stable him; Steve built a dividing wall out of wooden planks and actually made it into two stables. The shed was around the back of the farm and we thought it would not be nice to have one horse around there on his own, so we moved Guv and Smartie into the new stables, they were happy together, and as they were getting older, I think they liked the relative peace and quiet rather than the busy front yard.

It was nice having Duke back home; he and Harrie worked well together through the summer, they were popular with our guests and took some of the workload from Guv and Smartie. But neither Harrie nor Duke were suitable for novice riders, they were well trained high energy horses, and Duke would be leaving soon to go back to Coudelaria de Alter with Inês, therefore we had been thinking of buying another horse for the following season.

What we really needed was that 'one in a million' type of horse that anybody could ride, and that would be totally bomb proof. We often had families come for their holidays, where the mum and children rode regularly, but often the dad didn't ride at all, or only rode at a very basic level.

Guv had been my one in a million for many years now, but he was ageing. He had been a racehorse until he was nine years old and in the 1980's racehorses started work way too young; often they were racing at two years old, before their bones and muscles had fully grown. Guv was already showing signs of some arthritis and I didn't want him to have to carry heavier riders any more, he was too precious to me. We were not in any hurry; we had plenty of time over winter to search for a new horse before guests started arriving in early spring.

I spotted a beautiful horse advertised for sale near Lisbon. Craig was now old enough to look after the farm and all the animals for a few days, so we decided to have a mini break in Lisbon, and visit the owner of the horse at the same time.

Although we had been living in Portugal for nearly 10 years, we were relative newcomers to the delights of Lisbon. At heart, we were country folk with a farm full of animals to care for. Steve still worked in England for a few months each year, and I occasionally visited my family, who all lived in the Brighton area, but we had not been away on a holiday together since we arrived in Portugal. So, this trip was a real treat and I was feeling very excited about our adventure as we drove away from our farm.

We drove to Coimbra railway station, and left the car in a long stay car park, preferring to catch the train to Lisbon. Then we caught a taxi to our hotel in Lisbon's downtown region. History tells us that the Marquis of Pombal influenced the rebuilding of this part of Lisbon after the horrific earthquake of 1755. Our hotel was built inside one of these historic Pombaline buildings; the outside had retained many original features, but inside the hotel was modern and classy.

It was a complete contrast from the rustic country life that we were used to. The older clientele were very well dressed and opulent, making me aware of my country bumpkin appearance, but there were also some younger people staying, who were much more relaxed in their dress sense. The Portuguese are a very friendly nation, and everyone, from staff to other guests, wanted to share in our eagerness to explore their wonderful city. We were recommended a restaurant in the busy downtown streets which served traditional Portuguese delicacies enlivened by the cook's love of exotic seasoning. We both enjoyed our beef pica-pau with pickles, followed by a superb chocolate and chilli tart.

The next morning, we were up early and eager to see the sights. We had booked a three-hour walking trip with a guide, visiting Jeronimos Monastery, a Manueline and Gothic building from 1502. There was no expense spared on the building of this magnificent Monastery which houses the tombs of kings and famous explorers from Portugal's rich history. It is incredibly ornate, I cannot imagine how many sculptures surround the walls; it would take days to count them all. It was an amazing experience, and our guide Marco, who was so enthusiastic and informative, had lots more to show us.

He led us around the streets of Belem which lies on the banks of the Tejo estuary; we climbed up very steep narrow steps to the top of the tower, where I learned about Portugal's maritime exploration and navigational history dating back to the 13th century. I now have huge respect for the brave Portuguese adventurers of earlier times, setting off into the unknown in beautiful wooden sailing ships.

We also visited a 100-year-old cake shop which baked the famous Pasteis de Belem. These Portuguese delights are sold all over Portugal and called Pasteis de Nata, but this shop was their birthplace, and here they are still made to the original recipe. There was a long queue to buy these pastries, but as we were on a guided tour, it seemed that we could jump the queue, which I was very pleased about as my feet were starting to hurt! We found a place to prop ourselves outside the shop, and sat people watching for a while. The pastries were delicious, and the sugar hit replenished my energy reserves enough for me to finish our tour. We thanked our wonderful guide Marco, and took his recommendation on another excellent restaurant, before making our way back to our hotel to chill out for the rest of the evening!

Next morning, we jumped on a tram which took us through the picturesque mediaeval streets and squares. It's a great way to admire the architecture of this beautiful city. Portuguese azulejos (painted tiles) are a passion of mine, and in Lisbon there are many public buildings, palaces and churches where you can see this unique ancient art form decorating the walls. There are some famous azulejos depicting battle scenes, with men in full armour riding Lusitano horses, the artist even managing to capture the fear in the horse's eyes. Another popular historic subject painted on azulejos depicts ancient Portuguese sailing ships, at war on rough stormy seas: true works of art.

I had walked my feet off in the last two days, I don't think I have ever walked so far in my life, but it had been worth it, I was in love with Lisbon and it had made me realise how much I enjoyed travelling. We must take the time to occasionally leave our little paradise and see more of Portugal: but now I had to go and ride a horse.

Just before we had left home, I had received an email from a couple who we had met on a few occasions. When they had first arrived in Portugal from the US, they visited us to ask for information on vets, farriers and hay deliveries. They had already bought four Lusitano horses and were keen to breed top quality Lusitanos for the US market. We had helped them as much as possible; they lived over an hour from us, but I managed to persuade my lovely hay man Antonio to drive 400 bales of hay down to them. It was way out of his area and I think he only did it as a favour to me. Anyway, as I said, I received an email with a photo of a rather scruffy man in muddy wellingtons, sitting bareback on an equally scruffy horse which was for sale. The horse did look to be a beautiful dun colour, but so caked in mud that I couldn't be sure. I had completely forgotten about the email as our trip to Lisbon unfolded.

We were now heading towards Cascais, where Zorro, the horse that I had booked to ride, and possibly buy was stabled. I had spoken to the owner on several occasions and she had assured me that the horse was an easy ride and could be ridden in a simple snaffle bit. She had sent me a dozen photos, and in every one the horse was being ridden in a Pelham bit, which is a much stronger bit that should only be used by experienced riders. This should have been enough for alarm bells to have rung in my brain, but Zorro was so beautiful that I blocked the bells out!

As we approached the stables, the owner was already tacking up the horse in a pelham bit. After formalities which included me cooing over this stunning beast, I mentioned that I would like to ride Zorro in a snaffle bit. She looked horrified saying.

"Oh no, I never ride him outside of the arena in a snaffle." I knew Steve was fuming and was thinking that it had all been a waste of time, but I wanted to try this horse and judge for myself. The owner also told us that someone else had more or less agreed to buy him, so we were second in line. She was happy for one of her staff to take me out for a ride but only in the Pelham bit.

I really wanted to ride him so I agreed, and we set off. The sea air was crisp and as we headed for the cliffs, Zorro was really on his toes, he was enjoying himself and so was I.

"Would you like a canter?" shouted back Jasmine, her voice being blown away by the stiff sea breeze.

"Yes, please," I shouted, with a huge grin on my face. It was so exhilarating to be cantering along the top of the cliffs overlooking the Atlantic Ocean. Zorro was a beautiful horse, but he was strong in my hands, I kept trying to remind myself that I was looking for a horse that anyone could ride, even non-riders; and that certainly was not this beauty….but I allowed myself to dream….just for a little while.

We were staying the night in Cascais and returning home the following day. For lunch we stopped at a beautiful beachside restaurant, and ordered their speciality called Francesinha, a Portuguese sandwich, which the waiter told us originated in Porto, but was now enjoyed all over Portugal. It was made with bread, wet cured ham, linguica, sausage, steak, then covered with melted cheese and a hot thick spiced tomato and beer sauce was poured over the top. This mountain of stodge was then crowned with a fried egg. It was the most unappetising plate of food I have ever sat down to eat! We were starving, so resorted to picking out some of the best bits of meat; the restaurant was right on the beach front, so the view was lovely, as long as I didn't look down at the mess on my plate! We then spent the afternoon paddling in the sea, eating ice cream, and marvelling at the grandeur of the town. Cascais had been a little fishing village until King Luis I and the royal family made it their seaside residence in the 1870s. This attracted members of the Portuguese nobility to build grand villas, museums and parks. The beach we were enjoying was called Praia de Rainha (Queen's beach) and was where royalty would swim in its secluded and safe waters.

I had enjoyed my trip and although I was disappointed that Zorro was not a horse for us, I had to put our business first and not my own personal choices. I still had my darling Roxy, and all my other wonderful horses, but one day I would like to own a horse like Zorro.

We took the train back up to Coimbra where we had left our car. On the journey, Steve asked what I had thought of the horse in the email that we had been sent before we left home. I hadn't actually thought about him at all, but now Steve was looking at the picture, which he had printed from the email, and saying that he looked like a nice steady strong horse. No airs and graces but good and solid. I had to agree that he was right.

"William (the owner) only lives about an hour from Coimbra, we could pick up the car and drive down to see him. What do we have to lose? Shall I give him a ring and see if he is at home?" urged Steve. I knew he liked this horse, so I agreed.

"Yes OK, let's give William a ring."

Luckily for us William was at home and willing for us to visit. The horse now standing in front of us looked a totally different animal to the one we had seen in the photo. He was the colour of creamy custard, with a fine silky coat and a black mane and tail. Not a speck of mud in sight! William told us the background of the horse. He was a Lusitano, but bred for stock work rather than dressage. He had been used for rounding up sheep and general farm work.

I rode him into William's arena; he was such a comfortable horse to ride, and so easy to steer, just the slightest touch on the reins and he would turn, stop, go forward and also backwards. He had the smoothest trot that I had ever known, it really was not necessary to rise in the saddle at all, his canter was the same, gentle and unhurried. I got the feeling that this horse would always be happy to go down a gear, which was a great confidence giver for novice or nervous riders. William was happy for me to ride him out around the country lanes alone. I had never known such an accommodating horse. He was great and just what we needed. He would not have been my first choice if I was looking for a horse for myself, but I was not, I was looking for a horse for my business; he was perfect and his name was Domino.

CHAPTER 13

MAX

William brought Domino to our farm the next day in his trailer, and he settled in remarkably well. A few days later, I put up some small jumps in our arena and found out that he jumped effortlessly in his normal unrushed, unhurried way. His jumping was very calm and precise, he would be perfect for teaching people, because he only jumped what was in front of him; he didn't try to leap too high or approach the jump too fast.

We were expecting guests: Colin and Gill had been to us a couple of times before, so we knew them well enough to give hugs on their arrival. We were all hugging in our yard, happily chatting away when Gill suddenly shrieked over my shoulder "Domino!" and ran to his stable, a huge grin lighting up her face. Of course, I was quite shocked.

"Yes, it is Domino, how do you know him?"

"I rode him in the Alentejo (a region of Portugal) on a riding holiday. He was only 4 years old and wouldn't go across a stream. The leader of the ride tried to persuade him with her stick but he got more upset, so I decided to get off and lead him across. The stream was deeper than I expected and I got soaked" she giggled.

"Oh, that's a coincidence, we are crossing the river on our first ride tomorrow...do you want to ride him again?" I had planned to ride him myself, but after hearing Gill's story, I didn't fancy wet feet!

"You bet," she gushed, kissing his face, "Just try to stop me, I adore him!" Well, it seemed that Domino had found his first fan, and there were many more to follow.

A young family had recently moved to the area and start-ed riding with me. The girls, Bess aged 8, and Elva aged 12 years, had ridden Shetlands in Scotland for about a year so they knew the basics of riding already. Elva loved Duke, and always chose to ride him when he was living with us, and Bess loved Smartie. Pat, their mother told me that Bess talked about him constantly, and dreamed of him at night. Bess had a great love for horses even from an early age, and when Domino arrived, she fell in love with him too.

Later that summer, I was riding through the mountains with guests when we came across a very poor looking dog lying off the side of the track. If we hadn't been high up on horses, I wouldn't even have seen him. He didn't look up at us, or even try to move. We decided he must be waiting for his owner to come back, although it didn't seem likely as we were in the middle of nowhere. Two hours later, we thought we would retrace our steps and check if the dog was still there. Sure enough, he was. This time, I dismounted and went to see if he was ok. He had long curly black fur which was com-pletely matted up with gorse and brambles. I tried to get him to his feet but he was very unwilling and sunk straight back down again. He was very thin and weak. There was no way he would be able to walk home with us and he was too big to carry.

When we arrived home, Craig and I drove back in our trusty van, into the mountains, as close as possible to the spot where we had seen the dog. He was still there and in the same position. Again, we tried to get him to his feet, but he was too weak, it was as if he had given up. Craig carried the poor dog to our van and we took him home. We offered him water and he drank a little, we offered him dog biscuits but he didn't want to eat. I did manage to tempt him with a little bit of chicken but he just wanted to sleep. We made him a comfy bed and left him alone in a cool dark room. Tomorrow I would take him to the vet.

Next morning, he drunk water more readily, and ate some chicken, but he still looked at death's door. I tried to untangle the brambles and gorse from his fur and realised that he had quite a lot of bald thickened hard crusty patches on his skin. I thought it would be best to cut off as much hair as possible to make him more comfortable as we had done with Bastard Bun, and then take him to the vet. I was already feeling quite attached to him so you can imagine my shock when the vet said "This is a Portuguese Water Dog, if he has an identification chip, he will have to stay here while we contact his owner." Luckily he did not have a chip, so we were free to take him home. The vet said he had a very bad case of mange but he was too weak to treat at the moment as the treatment was very invasive. He gave me some high nutrient, easy to digest food and said it would be best to give him very small amounts regularly for a few days and then if he was stronger he would start the treatment. I did put up postcards in various shops and on the lamp post outside our house but I really didn't expect anyone to be looking for him. I was sure he had been abandoned.

I gently bathed his sore skin, and we tried a few doggy names to see if he responded to any of them and noticed that he did seem to respond a bit to the sound of letter x. Craig suggested Rex or Max and we settled on Max. A few days later, the vet gave Max the first dose of a very strong type of wormer. He told me not to hold on to his collar and after a minute, poor Max started throwing himself around the small room, howling as if in agony. I was so shocked, but the vet was calm, and within what seemed like an age but was probably only a few seconds, Max quietened. The vet gave me topical lotions for his sores and a shampoo to use weekly. He had to go back in three weeks for another dose of that awful medicine. How could I do that to him?

Over time Max recovered completely. He was a lovely dog, not young; the vet aged him at about ten years old. He had a bounce in his stride, more of a lope than a walk. I had never heard of Portuguese Water Dogs before, but now I had one, I was interested to know more.

They originated in the Algarve region but expanded all along the Portuguese coastline. They were excellent swimmers with webbed feet, capable of diving underwater to retrieve broken nets or herd fish. They would swim from boat to boat, carrying vital information in plastic or glass tubes in their mouths or tied to their collars, and their thick curly hair protected them from the cold Atlantic sea.

The breed almost became extinct in the 1960s, but has made a remarkable comeback, probably due to the fact that the Kennedys kept them and more recently President Obama had Portuguese

Water Dogs himself. They are now very fashionable, and I considered myself lucky to have the chance to own one, although there was one thing that struck me as strange....Max hated water!

My favourite cat, Misty, was acting strangely. She would take herself off for days at a time which was something she had never done before. She had lumps under her belly so I was expecting the diagnosis that the vet gave me. She had cancer. We were not sure how old she was, probably about 15 years. She had been born at our farm before we lived here. The former owner had given her to a young couple when she was a kitten, and she had lived with them for a number of years and had a few litters of kittens herself.

One day the young couple brought Misty and her daughter Tara around to us and asked if we would take them in, as they were going travelling. We reluctantly agreed but Tara never settled with us, she was petrified of our dogs, and every chance she got, she ran away. Eventually she returned to the neighbour of her former home, a journey of about five kilometres. Luckily the neighbour was happy for her to stay. Misty however, soon became the boss of our house, and I loved her. She had now been with us for about eight years, but her time was coming to an end, and I had to accept it. She didn't seem to be in much pain so the vet advised me to take her home and keep an eye on her, and when I felt she was ready, he would put her to sleep.

Misty and I had many special moments during her last two months. Our favourite was for her to lie on my tummy while I was in the hammock and we would rock together. She had always been a talkative cat and we had many conversations; putting the world to rights. Her beautiful eyes would look into mine and she would say "Miaw Miaw Miaw" and I would answer her "Miaw Miaw Miaw." Misty was a very sweet cat and is now buried under a Myrtle tree which has spectacular dark pink flowers that brightens our yard all summer.

Adam, the guy we bought our house from, had bought yet another ruin, although his life was based in England, he just couldn't stay away from Portugal. He loved it here, and had a lot of friends. He was a gregarious type of person and often made friends with other passengers on his ferry trips from England to Spain.

One man he befriended said he was interested in exploring this area of Portugal, so Adam gave him our phone number as a contact for him as he didn't have a phone line at his house. The first we knew of this was when our phone rang one morning. Steve picked up the phone and looked a bit taken back! After his conversation he explained to me that the guy had spoken in a very slow lazy drawl and said:

"Hey man, my name's Barry....I met Adam on the ferry and he said I could crash at his place for a while and that you would give me directions. I'm at the Spain/Portugal border at the moment." Steve obliged and gave him directions to Góis and told him to ring back when he got there, as the last bit of the journey was quite complicated.

We forgot all about this interlude and got on with our day. Later that afternoon, we got another call from Barry.

"Hey man, I must have missed the turning for Góis, I'm in Coimbra." Steve guessed where he had gone wrong, and directed him back onto the road towards Góis. Late that evening, the phone rang: Steve and I looked at each other, and sure enough...

"Hey man, I'm back where I started in Spain!" Finally, the next morning, he found Góis.

Now... the telephone box in Góis was rarely emptied of money, and when it was full it was impossible to put your money into the slot. Steve heard the 'beep beep beep' from the telephone box as Barry tried to put his coins into the blocked slot.

"I bet that's Barry at the phone box in Góis," he chuckled. At that moment, Adam pulled down the drive in his car and Steve told him the story. The phone was ringing again...beep beep beep!

"Oh, I suppose I had better go and pick him up" Adam conceded, and we thought we had heard the last of Barry.

A couple of days later, there was a knock at our door.

"Hey man, my name's Barry, I've fallen out with Adam, can I crash here for a while?" He was very tall and stick thin; with long greasy hair and an unwashed smell about him.

"My van is full of photographic equipment, if you have somewhere dry, that I can store it, I can sleep in my van." For the sake of my bed linen, I agreed to this immediately, and showed him a dry part of our shed. He unloaded his van and then sat down under my olive tree and rolled the biggest joint I had ever seen! The smell from the smoke was enough to get me high, so I left him there and continued with my horsey jobs.

After a couple of days, I asked him when he was leaving. He took offence and drove off, a joint dangling from his lips. He left all of his photographic equipment behind so I assumed he would come back for it. But he never came back, until.....

.....About a year later, his unmistakable rusty old van pulled down our driveway. Barry unfolded from the driver's seat, his long hair dangling down, and from the passenger side, a young woman with a grizzling child of about two years old emerged.

"Hey guys," came the familiar slow drawl "I'm back to pick up my stuff, is it ok if we crash for a couple of days, we're exhausted?" The young woman looked gaunt and anxious and the little girl was red eyed and had a streaming nose. How could I say no? I led them out onto the veranda and offered them some bread and cheese while I went off to make a pot of tea. When I returned, both adults were rolling joints, while the child munched hungrily on bread and cheese.

I introduced myself, seeing as Barry wasn't going to.

"Hi, I'm Sandra, are you hungry?"

"Hi, I'm Mary and this is Jessica, thanks for the food, we haven't eaten for hours." I asked them where they had been sleeping, and they pointed to the small van.

"We have been sleeping rough for two nights and have hardly slept at all." I could gladly have turned Barry away, but Mary and Jessica looked so desperate that I told them I would make up a sofa bed for the night. They were grateful, but the next morning, I couldn't believe the carnage.

Neither adult had any control over little Jessica, she was running around barefoot, and had obviously been through my cupboards as there was a broken marmite jar on the floor. Marmite was very precious to us as we could not buy it in Portugal, but more to the point, the little girl was running around in the broken glass. There were torn open bread rolls and butter splatters on the floor. It looked like this little tot had tried to make her own breakfast on the floor amongst the broken glass. There was no sound from her parents; they had slept through all the chaos and I, muggins, had to clear up all the mess before Jessica hurt herself!

Her parents paid her very little attention, so she began to follow me around everywhere, but it was dangerous to have such a small child with no sense of danger and no parental control around the horses. I tried my best, she loved to help me feed them, and I sat her up on their backs, but by the end of the second day, it was me who was exhausted! I told them that they would have to leave as I had guests arriving and needed their bed. This was not strictly true, we did have someone arriving, but he was not a paying guest and he would not be sleeping on our sofa.

They took the hint and Barry filled the back of the van with his photo equipment, he said he had a photo shoot in the Algarve, so they were leaving anyway. I hoped he did have some work, and the family could settle somewhere. I wished them good luck, and they were gone.

Francisco was approaching me as I was waving them off, his enxada slung over his shoulder. He wore his jute cloak with his hood up so that all I could see was his long, bushy, grey sideburns that merged into his equally bushy moustache. He stopped to chat, and his lovely liquid brown eyes looked solemn as he warned me that a storm was coming. He was off down to his field to weed his onions.

An enxada is a tool that Portuguese use for everything, it's a hoe, a fork and a shovel all rolled into one. His old jute cloak was also a common sight in olden times. Made from a heavy material, it kept the farmer warm and dry during showers and cold weather as they bent over their work, digging or tilling the ground. Francisco also used his cloak to wrap up long grass that he had scythed to take home for his goats. I got the impression that it was nearly as old as he was, in fact it could have been handed down from his father! Jute cloaks were common when we first came to Portugal, but these days, hardly anyone wears them anymore, preferring lighter weight modern materials.

CHAPTER 14

BRIDGE OVER THE CHURCH SPIRE

Paul, my eldest son, was coming with his new girlfriend for a holiday. He had told me lots about Natalie; he seemed to be captivated by her, so I was looking forward to meeting her. She was everything he had told me, charming, witty and full of energy; they were the perfect match. At one of the local swimming spots on the river in Góis, there was a tall tree with a bough that hung over the river. Paul and Craig climbed the tree with some of the other local lads, and jumped from the bough, making a huge splash. Natalie, not to be outdone, climbed up after them and made a spectacular jump into the fathomless water. Everyone, including me, clapped in appreciation. She was the only girl to dare to climb the tree.

"I know a place where there is a much higher jumping point" exclaimed Craig, always keen to impress his elder brother. I knew exactly where he meant. It was the gorge where, as I have already described, the river flows between two huge rock faces, forcing it to narrow and deepen, perfect for high jumping.

The next day, we all packed up a picnic and headed for the gorge. While Steve and I went for a relaxing swim, the three intrepid explorers set off to climb the side of the rock face, heading for an outcrop of rock that hung out over the river, about 12 metres from the surface of the water. I had seen Craig jump from this height before, but what about Paul and Natalie? Craig jumped first, he was waggling his legs about, showing off, but he hit the water straight and we all whooped as he surfaced and shook the water from his hair. He was treading water and shouting instructions to the two nervous daredevils standing above him. Paul let out a Tarzan like shriek and flung himself from the safety of the ledge. He landed well, and now we were all looking up at Natalie, who was looking decidedly petrified. We all shouted encouragement but she remained teetering on the edge of the narrow ledge. I opened a bottle of cold white wine and held up the glass to her.

"Go for it, Nat! Jump, or I will drink your glass of wine!" Natalie had taken a liking to Portuguese Vinho Verde, and this was enough to tip her over the edge…literally! Bravely, she pinched her nose, and launched herself into the abyss.

A few days later, we visited a dam where many years before, a whole village had been flooded. Sometimes at the end of summer, when the water level was at its lowest, you could see some of the flooded houses still standing. A little way up river, Paul spotted a bridge spanning the dam. It was about 25 metres high. He had been exhilarated since jumping from the rock, and was now eyeing the bridge speculatively.

"No, Paul!" I cried in alarm, "That is just too high, and someone told me that there is a church with a spire drowned down there somewhere." I was sure that this would be enough to put him off. But no, just before Paul and Natalie returned home to England, we were all invited to a party at our friend's house. It was a stone's throw from the dreaded bridge. Paul announced his plan to jump from the bridge that afternoon. He had brought Steve's wetsuit and was already changing into it. There was a buzz of excitement in the air as all of the partygoers walked with us to the bridge. We were blocking the road, and a couple of passing cars also stopped to watch the spectacle. Natalie and I were still trying to dissuade him, but he was adamant and climbed over the railings. He was standing there, meditating and preparing himself, when a young English guy called Pat, stepped over the railings, already stripped down to his boxers, and said "I'll keep you company…after three?" Paul grinned and nodded.

"One…two…three…" and they both jumped together. It seemed such a long time before we heard the splashes, and saw both heads bob to the surface. I realised that I had been holding my breath and I needed to cling on to Steve for support. We all walked over the bridge to the other side, and onto the shore.

Whooping with joy, Craig ran to meet them both as they emerged from the water, but they both seemed to be dazed, and almost staggered out of the water. I was worried, thinking that they were in shock and needed medical assistance, but they both insisted that they just needed to sit quietly for a few minutes. Paul had hit the water slightly crooked and was hurting all down one side of his body. As he slowly peeled off his wetsuit; we could already see bruising starting to appear. Pat seemed worse; he had pain in his spine, and also hydraulic problems!

"What was I thinking of, jumping from such a height in just my boxers? I've been really stupid and I think I'm going to pay for it" murmured Pat miserably.

Next morning, Paul and Natalie were leaving us, and after a very fretful sleep, Paul emerged with awful looking bruising all down one side of his body. He was cheerful enough, and said he was happy to lie in the hammock and let Natalie do all the packing. She had also offered to drive to the airport

"I'll have to jump from high bridges more often," he quipped, enjoying all the attention.

Poor Pat was not so lucky; he suffered some compression of his spine, and the doctor could not give a definite answer as to how well he would heal. Only time would tell.

CHAPTER 15

APOLLO

I had decided to send my lovely young horse Apollo to private school! He showed such talent for dressage that I thought it was worth spending some money to have him professionally trained. He would be away for two months, and I could only visit him once a week as it was a long drive to the training yard. I would miss him a lot, he had been born here, and I had a strong affinity with him. I understood his nervous nature which he had inherited from his mother Tessie, who had been badly treated and was mistrustful of humans.

Apollo's trainer was a young woman called Catarina. She was softly spoken and patient, which was an asset she would need to bring him to his full potential. I hoped they would get along together; I felt really bad about leaving Apollo, I couldn't tell him what was happening, or reassure him that I wasn't abandoning him.

I had experienced similar emotions when Craig had first attended school in Portugal. He had been only nine years old and was the only foreigner in the school. He didn't speak Portuguese and only one of the teachers spoke a little bit of English. I felt as though I was deserting him as he begged me not to send him into the classroom, yet now, he was a happy bilingual teenager, who was very well integrated into our local community. Sometimes you have to let go.

Catarina advised me not to visit for the first two weeks, to allow Apollo to settle in with her routine. It was torture for me; but eventually the day of my first visit arrived. I couldn't believe his transformation from mountain horse to dressage contender, in just two weeks! His coat, often mud splattered on our farm, shone like black satin and he looked really smart with his mane and tail plaited. On hearing my voice, he nickered a welcome, recognising me before he caught sight of me. I hugged him as he nuzzled my pockets, searching for the minty smelling treats hidden in there.

I led him out into the arena and Catarina mounted him. She had already explained the work that they had been doing together, and added that he had been a good pupil so far: intelligent and quick to learn. I could see that he was building up new muscle in his neck and hind quarters, he looked stunning and I felt very proud of him. The work he had learned so far was very basic, just walk, trot and canter transitions. We had done all of these lessons at home already, but now he looked much more relaxed and balanced, his ears were twitching, listening to Catarina's commands, not only with her voice but through her hands and leg movements. She asked him to stop by pushing her weight down into the saddle; he responded immediately and came to a perfect halt.

"Would you like to ride your horse? I can teach you both together if you like, it will make it easier for you to carry on teaching him when he goes home."

"Yes, that's a great idea, but I'm what we call in England, a 'Happy Hacker'. I've only ever had a few dressage lessons and they were a bit of a disaster."

"Oh, why was that?" Catarina wanted to know.

"Well, I thought my instructor was paying me a compliment when he said in his heavy German accent.

"Sandra; you ride like someone out of the TV show Dallas".

"Oh thank you" I replied, imagining that he meant I looked elegant and stylish, like one of the beautiful women from the series. Catarina smiled as if she knew what was coming next.

"'No" he shouted, "I mean that you ride like a cowboy"

"Oh well, that was me shot down in flames! My instructor had taken off my saddle and finished up the lesson with me riding bareback."

"There: see where your legs naturally fall when I take the saddle away?" he had shouted.

"And he was right, without the stirrups for support; my legs naturally fell straight down, so that if the horse was removed I would have landed on my feet." Catarina was nodding.

"He sounds like a good instructor."

"Well, I can't tell you how much I ached the following day, but I did go back and have a few more lessons with him, before he moved back to Germany. I hope I didn't drive him away!"

"You need to buy yourself a good dressage saddle, the one I am using will help to keep your legs in the correct position." She was right; I couldn't believe the difference it made. Something else for my wish list! Apollo continued to improve, but after two months, the cost of keeping him in livery and training was too much for us, so he came back home. He had learnt a lot and so had I.

I loved him so much that I have to admit, not many people rode him, I kept him for myself as much as possible. Roxy was my first horsey love, and always would be, but the two horses were so different. Roxy was bossy and naughty, but very funny; he still made me laugh with his behaviour and antics. Even though he was 20 years old, he could still spin 360 degrees when he got excited out on rides, and jog all the way home, which could be exhausting, but was good for my tummy muscles!

Apollo was totally different; gentle, sensitive and needy. When our farrier came to put new shoes on the horses, Apollo became nervous and fidgety. I had to stand at his head and soothe him, making a blinker with my hand to cover his eye so that he could not see the farrier working, then he was fine. It was the same scenario with our vet: Apollo needed me and of course that drove me to love him more.

We were expecting friends from the Isle of Bute in Scotland. They had friends who wanted to come for a riding holiday, staying in our cottage, and our friends decided it would be a good idea if they came too. Their three girls all loved to ride, and so did the two daughters of their friends. They were all flying out together; it was going to be a manic week! Our friends were Andy and Joan and their three daughters: Amy (22) Lizzie (19) and Lucy (13). Amy had a little two-year-old boy called Lewis. Their friends were Jonathan and Patsy, and their two girls Susan and Jessie, who were 12 and 14 years old. They would be staying in our cottage as paying guests. Our friends would be sleeping on the sofa bed in our lounge room, with Amy and Lewis sleeping on a mattress on the floor. Lizzie and

Lucy were sleeping in a tent outside. They couldn't sleep in the caravan because Mella and Simon were already staying there. We were full to the gunnels!

The girls were all keen riders; the others just wanted a chilled holiday. The horses worked hard that week, and so did we, but we had a lot of fun too, spending hours just paddling and chatting down by the river. Little Lewis was happy trying to catch the hundreds of tiny fish swimming close to the edge. Andy and Joan were old friends, Andy played guitar, and we spent long evenings on our veranda singing along to old Neil Young songs.

We reminisced about the past; we had once enjoyed a holiday with them, long before we came to Portugal. Back in the days when money was short, one of Andy's friends had offered him a week's holiday in his seaside 'shack' as he called it. In reality, it was an old converted railway carriage, there were a few of them scattered along the Sussex coastline; in fact my dad had been born in one, in a village called Selsey Bill, further along the coast.

We hadn't planned to have a holiday at all, Paul and Mella had gone on holiday with their father, as they had done every year since our divorce six years before. Steve and I had planned to have a quiet week at home, but when Andy phoned and invited us to join them at his friend's surf shack on the beach at The Witterings near Chichester, we spontaneously agreed, packed up the car, and went to the beach! It was one of our most memorable holidays. The old converted railway carriage was situated right on the beach; there was just a narrow pedestrian walkway between us and the shore. There were two bedrooms for the adults and a bunk room for the children. Craig and Amy were about five years old, and Lizzie was just a toddler of about two. Lucy hadn't been born.

The floors were old pine floorboards, easy to sweep up the sand that was constantly falling from our bare feet. There were no luxuries, the furniture was old, and we didn't have to worry about children with sticky fingers! Craig and Amy ran wild that week; they would be up early, and out onto the beach, as free as birds. Steve and Andy windsurfed whenever there was enough wind. I also enjoyed windsurfing, but was not as experienced as them, so only sailed when the wind was gentle. At other times they fished for our tea; I particularly remember Steve cooking crispy goujons for our lunch, with fish caught straight from the sea....delicious. Craig and

Amy searched the beach for driftwood, and in the evenings we lit a fire on the beach, with Andy strumming on his guitar as the stars appeared. We were only about 30 minutes from our home, yet we could have been anywhere in the world.

Now they were on holiday with us in Portugal: life changes, but good friends don't. Andy and Joan wanted to go to the Portuguese coast, so a convoy of five cars set off to our nearest coastal town of Figueira da Foz which has wonderful long sandy beaches, and is known for its huge surging surf. We strolled along the wide promenade paved with small, flat, black and white stones shaped into different mosaic patterns. Mature palm trees gave welcome shade, as we cooled ourselves down with some delicious home-made ice cream from a beachside cafe.

Figueira da Foz was built next to the mouth of the river Mondego, at the point where it flows out into the Atlantic Ocean. The river is 234 kilometres long; starting its journey high up in the Serra da Estrela Mountains, which are the highest mountains on mainland Portugal. Although Figueira now has city status, there are still parts that hold on to its original fishing village history. You can still watch the local boats come in to the beach with their haul of sardines. These small boats are colourfully painted with a very high bow to punch through the Atlantic waves. The men row the rearing boat out through the huge breaking surf, before starting up their motor and heading out to sea. When they return after a few hours, there are women on the beach waiting to slice open the sardines, and peg them out to dry on racks in the sunshine. These salted dried sardines are a Portuguese delicacy, and of course every restaurant serves freshly caught sardines, which we were just about to order for our lunch. We spent the afternoon lounging on the soft, warm sand, and playing and jumping over the frothy surf, which was much tamer now that it was low tide.

On another day, the same convoy drove up to the top of our highest mountain called the Serra de Estrela. At just under 2000 metres in height, the scenery and views are stunning. During the winter the peaks are covered in snow and it is a popular ski resort for Portuguese people. On this summer's day, the air was much cooler than down in the valley, and we all set off for a brisk walk. Little Lewis soon tired, he was only two years old, but there were plenty of men with broad shoulders to give him a ride, and we all helped to carry the basketfuls of food and drink for our picnic. We came across a waterfall, its cold water cascading down into a clear pool…the perfect picnic location. Because of the plentiful water, trees were able to grow in this harsh rocky environment and gave us welcome shade. Young and not-so-young took to the water with lots of splashing and squealing: it was freezing!

We drove back down the long winding road as the sun was setting over the landscape. White cumulus clouds had risen over the horizon and were painted with ever changing rays of colour. Our convoy wound its way into the valley below as twilight, in her timeless fashion, threw her veil over the sky.

About a week later, Steve and I were enjoying the peace of our now empty, quiet, house. I was leaning over the veranda watching the horses graze below us. Apollo was standing awkwardly on three legs, holding his front left leg out in front of him, but not putting any weight on it. Something was wrong; we both ran down to the field, and sure enough Apollo had a large rusty nail stuck in the centre of his hoof. These fields that bordered the river had been worked for centuries by farmers. The fields had water on both sides, so any crop would grow lush and quickly. On this stretch of the river, farmers had grown, and still were growing maize. Our field had not been used for planting for over twenty years, but before that, it would have been regularly ploughed by oxen, so there was a possibility that this nail had been part of an ox cart many years before.

It was definitely an ancient nail; it looked as though it had been buried for a hundred years. The flakes of rust were all peeling off, but it was still strong enough to have penetrated his hoof, right in the centre of his frog, which is an insensitive wedge shaped cushion, that helps the horse absorb shock. The health of the frog is vital to the soundness of a horse. Steve went back to the house to call the vet. His advice was to not remove the nail, but to try to keep Apollo calm, he was in the middle of treating a mare that was having a difficult birth, but he would come as soon as he could.

An hour later, our vet Diogo arrived. Apollo was incredibly nervous of vets, so it was a nightmare trying to hold him still while Diogo pulled out the nail, and packed the gaping hole with a dressing. Then we had to carefully lead him up the track to his stable, which was cleaner than the dusty field, and had access to clean water. He cleaned the deep wound with water and packed it with antibiotic dressing, then taped the whole hoof up so that no dirt could enter. He put an IV antibiotic drip into him, which would have to stay in overnight. I had a feeling that it wouldn't still be attached to him in the morning...and I was right, but hopefully enough antibiotics were released into his system to ward off infection.

Diogo returned the next day and repeated the treatment, but I could tell by his demeanour that he didn't hold out much hope. There was too much delicate tissue under the frog. Over the weeks, the hole grew over, but the internal damage to the navicular bursa was irreversible. Apollo would never be sound again. I was heartbroken.

Recently an Australian called Wayne had bought a house in a small mountain village quite near to us. He was a real character with mischievous blue eyes, a long silver-grey wizard type of beard and a long silver-grey pony tail. He walked with the aid of a stick, and although he seemed frail, he had a sparkle about him...a man of the world. He had lived in Denmark for many years and had developed an obsession with wood burners. Being a cold country, they make some of the best in the world. He had brought 28 different burners with him from Denmark and this was why we were meeting him; we needed a new wood burner. We didn't know that he had been a farrier and he didn't know that we had horses.

We entered a small room which was his living room; there taking pride of place was a Harley Davison motorbike, all black shiny metal and polished chrome. It was a thing of beauty: but in a living room? His bedroom was packed with wood burners, leaving just enough room for a single bed. Most were the excellent Jøtul brand, but my eyes fell on a black Morsø stove which had a large firebox on bowed legs with clawed feet. It had the capacity to take big logs and had a cooking stand on top; the firebox was decorated with a squirrel in a woodland setting, etched out of the iron. It was beautiful, and functional too. It was an antique, but was in good condition. We also needed a fire for the cottage, and I spotted a smaller Jøtul stove; it wasn't as decorative but it would be the perfect size to heat the cottage during the winter.

Wayne had an outdoor kitchen which had been just an old stone wall, but he had erected three posts about two metres out from the wall, and had laid a tiled roof.

"This type of roof, known as a lean-to in English, is called an uma agua (one water) in Portugal" Wayne told us.

"What has a roof got to do with water?" As I asked the question, the answer came to me. "Ah, of course; is it because water runs one way down the roof?"

"Yeah, you got it" answered Wayne.

"Our house is called a hip roof in English, so would that be known as a quatro aguas (four waters) here in Portugal?"

"I think so." He added pensively "There is a village called Quatro Aguas near here, I wonder how it got its name, I will have to make some enquiries."

He had a small fire burning in a grate, which he poked into life before filling his kettle, and placing it on the grate; he invited us to stay for a cup of coffee and to talk prices. His lovely old English bulldog wandered over to slobber on me.

A few metres away Steve had spotted an old wooden beam. He loved wood, and the two men wandered over to take a look. It seemed that as well as his motor bike and wood burners, Wayne had also brought over from Denmark a pile of his best wood. Needless to say, he had no wife! Wayne had named the old beam Bertha; Steve had already decided where she would be going, so it looked like Bertha was coming home with us as well as the two burners. Wayne promised to bring them round to our house the next day.

As Wayne climbed slowly out of his truck the next morning, he sniffed the air.

"You have horses" he said as he reached for his stick.

"Yes, we do." I answered, always happy to meet another horsey person. "Are you a horse lover? Would you like to meet them?" I asked, as I ushered him towards my pride-and-joys.

Wayne told us that he had been brought up with horses and had trained and worked as a farrier for many years in Sydney, until a stroppy mare had kicked him in the back and he had never fully recovered. As we were talking, he patted each of the horses and cast an experienced eye over each one. He stopped at Duke.

"This is a good horse, he has the look of an Australian stock horse, a good broad chest and four strong legs; I like him." Then his eye fell on to Apollo.

"Geez ...what happened here?" Apollo backed away from Wayne nervously, but Wayne just held out his hand, making no attempt to pat him, and after a few seconds, Apollo came forward and stretched out his neck to sniff Wayne's finger tips. Apollo moved another couple of steps forward and before long he was ducking his head, allowing Wayne to scratch behind his ears as I told him Apollo's story.

"Gee, that's sad, and he's young, isn't he?"

"Yes, he is just seven years old" I answered miserably.

"Well, as you can see, I can't treat him," Wayne said, leaning heavily on his stick. "But I may know a man who could help."

My heart leapt, he was throwing me an arrow of hope.

CHAPTER 16

BIG BERTHA

Wayne had used his neighbour's tractor which had a grabber attachment to load Big Bertha into his open topped truck, but now we had another problem...how were we going to get her out? I had been training Comet in the basics of long reining, and getting him used to pulling a heavy tyre behind him, because I thought that he could make a nice driving pony, and pulling something like a heavy tyre is a good way to start his education. I quite fancied myself sitting up in a little cart, with Comet trotting around the lanes. I could take him to the shop, park him outside, and buy large quantities of wine, potatoes, beer and heavy gas bottles. I could even teach driving to my guests.

We all had a discussion, and agreed to give Comet a go. I had already bought a neck collar for him, so I just needed to attach long ropes on either side of his body, and attach them to the chain that Wayne had fixed around one end of Big Bertha. Then I led Comet forwards so that he took up the slack and felt the pull on his collar from the heavy beam. He seemed completely unfazed so we walked a couple more steps and Bertha began to slowly move towards the back of the open truck, which was about 18 inches from the ground. Any second now there would be a big bump as the beam fell head-first to the ground. Still Comet showed no sign of fear, I hugged and kissed him, telling him how good he was, and we walked on another few steps until Bertha was completely clear of the truck and was lying on the ground. Now Comet just had to pull the beam over towards the cottage, which was where it was going to live. I was so proud of him, he was a little star.

The original plan for the cottage had been for one large mezzanine bedroom, but as soon as bookings for our riding holidays had started coming in, we realised that we had made a mistake. We were attracting many families and it became apparent that we needed two bedrooms. Steve had improvised and sectioned off an area of the original bedroom to make a second bedroom out of plasterboard. He had never been happy with the outcome and had always planned to one day build a better second bedroom. This was what he planned to use Big Bertha for. She would be the main joist, taking the whole weight of smaller joists that would hold up the second bedroom. Now we just had to rustle up enough manpower to lift her up there! This was easily done with a phone call to a few friends, telling them to bring their friends to a pipi piri chicken barbeque, with plenty of cold beer. We had so many volunteers, that we could have lifted two Berthas!

Wayne was true to his word, and sent our x-rays of Apollo's hoof off to his old colleague Harry in Sydney, who was a remedial farrier. He treated the best racehorses and show jumpers in the country, people sent their horses to him from all over Australia. He and Wayne had been friends since college days, and Wayne was sure that he would be happy to look at the damage done to our little horse's hoof, and give us any advice that he could. Harry studied the ex-rays and took the time to gather other vets and farriers together, and come up with what we all hoped would be a solution to our problem.

The experts all agreed that the deep digital tendon had suffered trauma and the bursa had been badly infected and was not likely to recover sufficiently. They thought it was worth trying to raise his heel up to relieve pressure. They gave an in-depth account of treatment that they hoped would help, and we followed it to the letter for the next six months. Apollo would need a high heeled shoe: Steve had the idea to ask our local car mechanic if we could use his welding equipment. He was a horse lover and enjoyed seeing our horses regularly trotting past his garage, so he offered to help Steve create a shoe with a heel. We had plenty of old used horseshoes, so they cut off four pieces of metal from an old shoe, and welded two of them together on each side of Apollo's shoe, raising it by 2.5cm. This would relieve pressure on his tendons, and hopefully allow them to heal.

Steve had been forced to do a crash course in farriery when we had first arrived in Portugal many years before. The only farrier we had been able to find was Henrique, an old man who shod the police horses in Coimbra. He was used to treating one or two horses a week, so although he was very experienced, he struggled to do all of our horses in one day. Steve had to help him; Henrique taught him to take out the nail heads and gradually loosen the shoe, until it could be pulled from the hoof. Then Henrique shaped the hoof using a huge nail file and banged in the nails, leaving Steve to cut off the protruding nail heads and file them down.

Henrique used to catch the train from Coimbra to our nearest station at Serpins, where we had to go and pick him up. Later we took him back to the station, exhausted, after he had shod our horses. Then the poor man had to cycle back to his home. It was quite a palaver, so if a horse lost a shoe while out riding, which does happen, it was too much to expect Henrique to come all the way just to fix one shoe. So, on quite a few occasions, Steve had actually nailed on horse shoes. At first it was really scary, but he was a carpenter by trade so he had a good eye, and so far all had gone well. It seemed amazing to me that in England, and I'm sure in other countries too, a farrier is well paid and respected, but this little guy rode his old bike to Coimbra station, and then caught a train to us. The tools of his trade were wrapped up in a carrier bag, and he wore ordinary town clothes and shoes!

Henrique had since retired and we had found a younger Belgian farrier to shoe our horses. He was quite amused when he saw our home-made shoe with a high heel, but he shaped the hoof and fitted the shoe, just as we asked him to. It seemed to do the trick, Apollo was standing and walking on his lame leg a bit easier, maybe there was a glimmer of hope. The experts had said that we must remove the shoe every month and lower the heel each time. So, with our car mechanic's help, Steve removed the shoe and lowered the heel by a small amount each month. We both hoped with all of our hearts that in six months time, Apollo would be walking normally without the aid of a raised heel, as this could never be a long term solution. He had been lame for 2 months, and standing on three legs was affecting his posture. His beautiful physique had disappeared, and I felt that he had pain in his back from constantly standing crooked.

Now that he was walking a little easier, I could take him out for walks, allowing him to graze on the lush grass along the roadside. He was such a sweet horse, he was never bad tempered even through his pain, but although I tried to keep thinking positive, deep down inside, my feeling of doom persisted.

We had been living in the mountains of Portugal for over ten years and were beginning to notice changes. In the past, in every small village, someone owned an ox and a mule or donkey. They would be used communally for ploughing and as haulage for bringing in the crops. One of our neighbours owned an ox, and a few times a year, he would lead it along to our yard, and leave it standing there while he and a group of others walked down a steep narrow track to the fields below our house, to chop down the ripe maize heads, and load them into buckets and baskets before carrying them up the steep track and emptying them into the cart. This repetitive work would go on all afternoon until the cart was full of corn cobs.

The huge ox was so gentle; he was a beautiful tan colour with long blonde eyelashes shading large inexpressive eyes. When the cart was full to overflowing, the ox was led up our steep driveway, his short strong legs almost buckling under the weight. One time, a rather large lady tried to jump on the back of the cart to hitch a ride and the poor ox could take no more. His front legs slipped under him and he fell onto his knees. There was no panic in the animal, no fear showed in his eyes, he was like a machine that had broken down, he just stayed as he was with his front legs trapped under his body and his back legs still standing.

We came running out of our house to see if we could help, but there was so much shouting and gesticulating, that I don't think anyone was aware of us. The cart was unhitched and the poor animal was helped to his feet. He seemed unhurt, and soon the cart was trundling home...minus the fat lady!

The corn heads would be fed into a hand turned machine that stripped the kernels, then the kernels would be laid out on huge plastic sheets to dry in the sun. Once dried, the kernels would be ground into flour, or crushed and fed to animals. This routine had been taking place for centuries; but times were changing. More people had nine-to-five jobs, and didn't have the time to carefully tend crops, and look after goats, chickens, and other animals.

Supermarkets were springing up. Whereas ten years ago, there had been one corner shop that sold more or less everything, and people grew a lot of their own produce, now supermarket chains were moving in and changing the way people fed their families. One morning, we heard a commotion in the fields below our farm. Each small plot of land was bordered by ancient grapevines, that had provided wine for the villagers, while the leaves and tendrils had fed the animals for millennia. Now a bulldozer was tearing out all of the vines, opening up the tiny patchwork of fields into one huge area. Francisco and a group of older neighbours had gathered to watch. He proudly told us that the village had decided to open up the fields so that a tractor could come and plough up the whole land.

As far as I knew, nobody owned a tractor and when I pointed this out to him, he tapped his nose and said that a man from Quatro Aguas had just bought an old Ford tractor. He was happy to travel the ten kilometres to come and plough their lands, as long as he could do it in one sweep, and not have to keep turning in tiny circles between grapevines. The villagers had all agreed; it would make their lives easier and they could grow more corn. Most of them had other pieces of land planted with grape vines, so they could still produce their own wine, but I was sorry to see the ancient vines ripped out of the ground. Francisco was in a jubilant mood and he couldn't wait to tell me why: he was to become a grandfather for the first time. I felt so happy for him.

Mella and Simon had been staying with us for a month. They both talked excitedly about moving out here to live full time which would be wonderful for me, but finding employment would be hard. Simon was an electrician, so maybe he would be able to find work here. He would need to learn the language, but any work was hard to find outside of the cities, and here in the mountains most folk seemed to be able to turn their hand to anything...even electrical work!

Mella was studying for her British Horse Society exams which would qualify her to teach riding in Portugal. Her dream was to work with me and expand our business. She was working for a British horse magazine, and couldn't afford to leave work and enrol full time in a college course, but thankfully the magazine offered to give her one day off a week to attend a BHS college course. This was a great help to her but what she needed was a horse of her own to practice with during the evenings and weekends.

I had recently signed up to work with a Swedish horse holiday company and we were already receiving bookings from them for next year. Something I noticed was that a lot of Nordic people were above our weight limit. We had a limit for riders of 90 kilos, but some of these new bookings were for people well over our limit. Most of our horses were now Lusitanos or Lusitano mixes, and our landscape was mountainous, so we would need a big strong horse to carry weights of up to 100 kilos day after day. Dutch Warmblood horses are big and strong and quite common in England, though not here in Portugal. We had been very impressed with Duke, who was a Dutch Warmblood, but he didn't belong to us anymore, and he was only here for three months in the summer when Inês, was on holiday from her college.

Mella knew of an importer who brought young horses over to England from Holland; he then trained them, and sold them on. I asked her to go and visit him, to see if he had a horse suitable for us. She phoned me that evening saying that she had found the perfect horse for us.

He was a big powerful chestnut, with a wide white blaze. His name was Ucarius and he was seven years old. Mella had already fallen for him; she called him her 'big teddy bear'. We bought him with a three-month warranty, and things went very well for the first two and a half months. Then for no apparent reason he became lame and was eventually diagnosed with navicular, which is a debilitating foot syndrome that rarely has a favourable prognosis. Mella contacted the dealer, and he said that she should bring the horse back and he would replace him with another one.

Mella asked what would happen to Ucarius (aka Teddy Bear) but the dealer wouldn't say. She was very upset and demanded to know. He said she could buy him for £500 and he would still replace him with another horse. She couldn't let him go; we both knew where he would end up, so she bought him. She couldn't afford to keep two horses, so his replacement was sent straight out to me.

Hero was a 17hh dark bay with a jagged long thin blaze that reminded me of the contours of Chile. He had white legs below the knee, and was a really striking German Holsteiner horse. He had a large frame, but was a bit thin. He would be a big strong horse in a year's time for sure. It seemed that he had been shipped from Germany to Holland, next stop England, and then straight out to Portugal. The poor lad seemed dazed and confused. He was only 5 years old, but dwarfed my stables. I think he was just happy to be on terra firma, and after a few days, his personality started to show. He was just a baby, very mouthy and a bit nippy and bolshy. His long neck could reach around the stable door to where his head-collar hung and he jubilantly grabbed it in his teeth and threw it across the yard; a bag of grooming brushes followed; the contents spilling out into the dust.

It was springtime so there was plenty of grass. I don't think he had ever been turned out into a field of grass; he was so excited, he didn't know whether to run around and buck, or scoff the grass, or roll on his back and throw his long legs into the air. He did all three, before settling to graze and enjoy the warm spring sunshine on his back. He did show the whites of his eyes which is supposed to be a bad omen, but I wasn't superstitious, and I liked him. As his weight improved and his energy returned, I started to lunge him daily. He seemed very well behaved, so after a week of lunging, I decided it was time to get on board.

It's always an anxious moment when you ride a young horse for the first time. I had no idea about the level of his education, or how much work he had done in Germany, but thankfully our first ride in the arena went well. He had a lovely long stride and seemed to know the basic commands for walk, trot and canter. He loved living within our herd, and was respectful and submissive to the other older horses. I had hoped for an older heavyweight horse, ready to work, but things don't always work out as you would wish, and he would be ready for next year; and hopefully many years to come.

During the summer of 2005, Portugal was ablaze. Our Central region was badly hit, smoke covered the sun and the air was thick with the acrid smell of charred wood. The dense smoke amplified the sunsets, making them appear more red than usual. It was an eerie and unsettling time, almost post-apocalyptic. My mother, brother and niece were visiting for my birthday in July, as well as my eldest son Paul and daughter Mella with her boyfriend Simon. My brother Richard was a photographer, and the plan was that he would take photographs of us riding our horses in the beautiful sunny Portuguese landscape for our new website. I was particularly keen for him to capture us trotting through the river, with water spraying up around us. But that clearly was not going to happen; the only thing spraying around us was charred eucalyptus leaves!

We didn't want to leave the farm because a single eucalyptus leaf, alight and floating on the breeze, could ignite a new fire anywhere. We had been staying home, filling every bucket that we owned with water, and had all of our hoses at the ready to attack any stray sparks. When I awoke at night, my first instinct was to sniff the air for smoke; it was an unsettling feeling, knowing that at any time, we could lose everything that we had worked so hard for.

On my birthday, the fires seemed to be more under control, and the air was clearing. Our yard was littered with ash and the acrid smell still clung to the air, but the sun had broken through, and we were all feeling less tense. We had not been in any real danger and had not been asked to evacuate as many villages had, but it had been close enough. My birthday celebration was to be held in a restaurant about 40 minutes' drive away. It had an outdoor swimming pool, surrounded by nice green lawns, littered with sun loungers where waiters served drinks and snacks. We all left in two cars in the early evening, with the hope of taking a swim and maybe a gin and tonic around the pool before dinner. It was a Brazilian restaurant and we knew the food was great, so this was to be a real treat....or so I thought.

We were about halfway there when we heard the first sirens and saw smoke billowing up into the early evening sky. The fire was leaping and spitting through a forest very close to the main road that led to the restaurant. I couldn't believe the speed it travelled in the fierce wind that had recently sprung up. It was as if the wind picked up the flames and tossed them in all directions, like an old-fashioned farmer sowing a field of corn. The bravery of the helicopter pilots, who were bombing the front edge of the fire with water, was phenomenal. Their helicopters actually disappeared into the billowing smoke to make sure they hit their target.

The road had been closed to traffic, but for a few moments we were mesmerised by the scene we were witnessing, before the police signalled to us to turn around and go back.

A convoy of fire engines, sirens blaring, raced into the thick smoke to reach the blaze. These fire-fighters are so incredibly brave...and they are volunteers! Many people owe them their lives. We tried different routes to reach the restaurant, but all routes were blocked. I remembered that we had been told good things about a restaurant in the town of Lousã, which was quite close by. We were all getting hungry so we decided to give it a try.

Our first impressions of the restaurant were not favourable although it was very easy to spot, it was bright yellow with black stripes. My brother started making the sounds of a buzzing bee, and named it the buzzy bee restaurant! Everything was in yellow and grey laminate. The strip lighting had yellow covers, the tables, chairs, and even the serviettes were yellow and grey stripes! I assume the owners thought it was modern and clean, but it had no charm at all. The yellow and grey tiled barbeque area was integrated into the restaurant, making it very stuffy on this hot July night. We all ate barbequed food, which was good, but not memorable. On the journey home we could see that the fire was still raging on the main road into Coimbra, I felt lucky to have a home and my lovely family around me, but during these hot Portuguese summers, the threat of fire is inextinguishable.

CHAPTER 17

HERO

Francisco's baby grandson was born; he was named Francisco, Chico for short. Right from the start it was as if Francisco had grown an attachment to his arm! He carried the baby everywhere. He told us proudly that the baby only slept when he was being rocked in his arms. He carried little Chico down into his field below our house, and with the baby lying on a blanket, we would hear Francisco whistling lullabies to the child as he tended his crops.

From a very young age, Chico loved the horses, he never showed fear as their huge heads sniffed his baby smell, and it wasn't long before he was tottering along the road at his grandfather's side, pointing his little finger and saying.

"'Valos,'valos, avô!" (Cavalos—horses, granddad)

As he got older, Chico liked to sit on Smartie's back, and pat him with his little fists. One day, Francisco passed by our house without Chico. This was so strange that I commented on it. Francisco looked crestfallen, Chico had been having breathing problems and after doing tests, the doctor discovered that Chico had an allergy to animal fur. When Francisco had mentioned that his grandson loved horses, the doctor advised him to keep Chico away from them, as it could be horses that were triggering his allergies. He cheered up enough to tell me that his daughter was pregnant again, so hopefully I would soon be hearing more lullabies.

Apollo's hoof was a little better, but he was still too lame to ride. I didn't mind, I was happy to keep him as a pet. One of our guests had been studying a training method that I had not heard of before, called the Parelli groundwork training. The idea is that you teach your horse respect and trust as well as mutual communication by playing games. It was almost like training a large dog! Apollo loved it and so did I, and it was something new to teach our guests. Groundwork was becoming more and more popular, with more people realising that it didn't always have to be about riding, you could have fun with your horse without getting on its back.

I was riding my new horse Hero out in the mountains, he behaved well at first, cantering in a line behind the more experienced horses, but as his confidence grew, he realised that he was much faster than some of the other horses, and galloping was great fun; especially overtaking! One day I was riding Hero out with Inês and Duke, we had been riding for about half an hour when we decided to have a canter. Hero got so excited that he just exploded on the spot, throwing in a huge buck that sent me flying over his head: I hit the ground hard on my head. My helmet cracked open from the impact and my elbow was at a very strange angle, but it was my vision that scared me most of all.

Everything was blurred. Inês jumped down from Duke and grabbed hold of Hero's reins, while I just sat dazed at the side of the track. Neither of us had a phone, so the only option was to walk slowly back home. Everything else seemed to be working ok, except my vision which was still very blurred, and a thumping headache. We made it home without further incident, and Steve insisted on taking me directly to A&E.

Coimbra has a fantastic hospital; I was sent straight away for a CT scan, and I was seen by a brain specialist within an hour. He spoke to me in English with a heavy Portuguese accent, and explained that my brain had been rattled! I couldn't help but chuckle, especially when he told me that I would need to wear an eye patch for a few weeks! He said that I needed to rest my eyes by swapping the patch from one eye to the other every hour, and I was not allowed to watch TV. Well, that stopped me chuckling—after living for over five years without electricity, I now loved my TV. He also clicked my dislocated elbow back into place, which proved to be the most painful part of the whole process!

I was concerned about what to do with Hero, I knew that he wasn't a horse for us, he was just too powerful, he was fine in an arena, but riding outside in the forest was too much of an overload of excitement for him, yet I was sure he had the ability to become a good dressage or jumping horse. I searched our meagre internet, and finally found someone who had a good reputation for training top class horses near Lisbon. We went to meet him. He introduced himself as Pedro, and said that German horses, and in particular the Holsteiner breed, usually had a talent for jumping, and were very sought after in Portugal. He offered to send his truck up to our farm to pick the horse up and he would start his training. I didn't know what else to do, the fees were astronomical, but it would be impossible to find him a good home here in the mountains, so I agreed.

After one month, we went to visit Hero, I had spoken to Pedro a few times on the phone, and he was happy with how Hero's training was going. He had spent the first three weeks teaching Hero respect and to listen to his rider. They had been concentrating mainly on basic dressage work, but Pedro had popped him over a few low jumps and proclaimed him a natural!

He told us that Hero really enjoyed his work, but he had seen some of the behaviour that I had told him about on occasions. Sometimes he had to share the arena with one or two other riders, and when this happened, he definitely noticed a difference in Hero's behaviour, saying that he became excitable and unfocused. Pedro put it down to his age, saying he was like a child that needed to grow up. Today we had the arena to ourselves, and Pedro had put up three jumps of about one metre. I was surprised to see how easily Hero jumped that height. He almost stepped over them!

"You see," shouted Pedro as he cantered around the arena. "I told you he is a natural."

Later, when Hero was back in his stable, enjoying his lunch, Pedro told us that he thought Hero had huge scope, and could become a top class show jumper in about a year's time. He said that John Whittaker, and other top British show jumpers, often visited his stables looking for young talent. We were very excited, but knew that our finances couldn't stretch to the cost of one year's training; however, we asked Pedro to carry on with his work, and if a buyer came along, to let us know. Two months later, we received an invite from Pedro to watch Hero at his first big event. It was to be held in the Algarve, and the course would be over 1.5metres.

The big gangly horse that had left my yard was now a stunning, confident, muscular powerhouse. He flew around the course, clearing every jump easily, ears pricked forward, and totally synchronous with his rider. A man approached us as we were still jubilantly clapping his clear round. He told us that show jumping was his passion, and he was looking for a horse for himself and his son to compete on. Show jumping was his hobby, a stress buster from his hectic hotelier business, but his son was passionate about horses, and would have the time to bring Hero to his full potential. He offered us 10,000 euros. We were gobsmacked! We had paid 3,000 for him, so even with Pedro's costs, it was a tidy profit! He said that he would be keeping Hero at Pedro's yard, and we could visit him whenever we wanted to. I felt happy for Hero; he would be doing what he had been bred to do. Some horses are just not suitable for trekking, and can become frustrated, bored and dangerous.

Once Hero was sold, I started looking on the internet at horses for sale; I was looking for a big strong horse capable of carrying weight, it was going to be hard to choose, but one morning, my eye was caught by the most stunning Lusitano horse. He was as black as thunder, so he was aptly named.... Trovão (Thunder) The advert was very well presented and featured a beautiful black horse with a long flowing black mane and tail, trotting through a throng of people, obviously at some sort of parade. The horse was being ridden by a man in full Portuguese riding costume. There was a fox skin attached to the back of the saddle, on which sat a beautiful woman, in a long dress.

The image captured me, and I was hooked! We contacted the owner who lived in Alcobaça which was about a two hour drive for us. His name was Rodrigo, and he told us that he worked every day and could only meet us in the evening. We arranged to meet him at a restaurant in the main square of Alcobaça, and by the time he finally turned up, it was dark. We had enjoyed a very nice meal at the restaurant while waiting for Rodrigo to arrive, so with full tummies, we followed Rodrigo to the yard where the horse was stabled.

Seeing Trovão in the flesh, my first thought was that he must be a stallion; he had such a big powerful neck. Rodrigo's German girlfriend, Carolina, was also present and explained that the 10-year-old horse had been a stallion until last year, when she had persuaded Rodrigo to have him castrated, so that he could have a better standard of life. Stallions have to be kept in secure stables as they will try to escape if there are mares in the vicinity; they are also more prone to fighting than geldings. By gelding Trovão, he would be able to spend time in a field with other horses, and enjoy his life. He assured us that as far as he knew, Trovão had never been used for breeding, which usually meant that he would adapt to losing his manhood much easier than a stallion that was accustomed to servicing mares each year.

Carolina led him out of the stable; he was absolutely stunning, he held himself so beautifully. Next moment, she jumped up onto his back and started riding him around the arena just by the light of the moon. She had no saddle, and rode him with just a halter and rope. He seemed very calm, but I would need to ride him myself outside of the arena, and I couldn't do that at night. I asked the couple if they would consider letting me take the horse on a month's trial period. This was common in England, but unheard of in Portugal. Rodrigo looked astounded.

"You are asking me to take my horse away, without paying me any money? No way! Do you think I'm mad?"

Luckily, Carolina stepped in.

"Let me talk to him," she interrupted. "Trial periods are common in Germany also." She took his arm, and walked a little way off. She was talking calmly, but Rodrigo was throwing his arms up into the air, shaking his head.

While they were turned away from us, I stood close to Trovão, stroking his neck, and he turned to gently sniff and nuzzle me. He reminded me of the only stallion I have ever owned. His name was Silver Moon; we had rescued him from a bad place, where he had been chained to a trough in a dark underground stable. The chain was so short that he couldn't even lie down. He was badly lame from a bullfighting injury, and the owner said we could take him as it would save him having to shoot him. We took Silver home and gave him his own stable, but he was nervous and institutionalised, and went straight to the back of the stable and stood with his head to the wall. Whenever I opened his door to feed him, he would never come forward for his bucket of food until I had left the stable. It was heartbreaking, but very slowly over time, he came to trust me, and one day when I approached with his food, his lovely head came over the door and he nickered a greeting and nuzzled me, just as this horse was doing now.

The couple walked back over to us, and Rodrigo reluctantly agreed to bring the horse to my farm for a period of one month. Trovão's hooves were in a bad way, his shoes were loose, and clattered on the concrete walkway as we led him back into his stable. I would need to have the farrier put new shoes on him before I could do any work with him, but in my heart, he was already mine. After only two weeks, I paid the money, I was very happy with him; he was just what I needed, a strong capable horse that was scared of nothing. His work as a parade horse meant that nothing fazed him; he felt wonderful to ride, and had a proud high stepping action, I was sure my guests would love him.

Our new group of guests had just arrived; three of them, Emma, Jayne, and Phil were sharing the cottage. They were friends from the same riding school, and my first impression was that they were going to be a lot of fun. We also had an older couple, Frank and Julie, who had booked to stay in our guest bedroom. My first impression of them was slightly different! After I had showed them to their room, Frank said in a rather hard-edged voice.

"The website says, 'as much wine as you can drink!'"

"Ah yes," I replied, "would you like me to bring you a jug of wine?" He nodded, and went to use the bathroom. I made a mental note to myself to change the wording on the website to something like 'Wine flows freely at meal times'!

At dinner that night, he was a little 'jolly', but not too bad, and we all had a good evening getting to know each other. Jayne was obviously the joker of the group, and next morning when I allocated them all with the horse I thought most suitable, Jayne piped up and said that she wanted to ride Roxy! I warned her that he could be a bit crazy, but she just replied that she was crazy too and had already bonded with him, playing "Bite me if you dare," over the stable door. Frank was to ride Harrie, which he was very pleased about, and his wife Julie would ride gentle Guv. Emma had already chosen Smartie, and I agreed that they were a good match. Phil was the least experienced, so I offered him Domino, who was my most steady, reliable horse, but he asked if he could ride Comet, explaining that he would have to dismount regularly and walk for a while as his hips were not good and Comet was small enough for him to mount easily from the ground. Phil was small and light-weight so I agreed, but only on the condition that he was willing to walk up some of the steeper hills to help Comet out. He was happy to do that, and as the week went on, Comet and Phil formed a real bond. I rode Trovão; it would be his first week out in a group, but I already had great confidence in him.

The three young riders were very animated and great fun to ride with, the older couple seemed happy to stay behind, which was fine by me. Frank and Julie both looked as if they were good riders, in complete control of their horses, so imagine my shock when on the first canter, which was on quite a narrow track, and I had asked everyone to stay in single file, Harrie and Frank galloped past me! Emma had screamed out that Frank had nearly knocked Smartie off of the track, she was very upset, and I didn't blame her.

"Did you lose control of Harrie?" I asked Frank, worriedly.

"No, of course not," he replied laughing, "That was great!"

"Frank", I said, as calmly as I could, "you can't just gallop past the other horses on these narrow tracks, it's dangerous, you will have a chance for a gallop later on a wider track." Frank didn't an-swer, he was still in the lead of the group, and I had a feeling he was angry at being reprimanded; I didn't feel in control of the situation. I was just about to ask him to take Harrie to the back of the group, when he turned his horse around and headed back to his wife. I could feel his fury.

Later, we reached a wide, long, ridge track where it was safe to have a fast gallop. I called Frank and Julie to the front, and asked Frank if he would lead the gallop. They were on the fastest two horses anyway, I thought this would please him, and it did!

At lunch there was a slight atmosphere, but the three younger guests were in jubilant moods, so it went unnoticed. Frank drank nearly the whole litre of wine that I had put on the table, and asked for a refill to take to his room. We didn't see him again until about 5 pm, when Julie said that they were going for a walk. Frank stag-gered through the yard, he didn't look at all steady on his feet, and within five minutes they were back.

At dinner that evening, we were all chatting together on the veranda, when we heard a thump, and looking towards Frank, we saw that he had fallen asleep on his dinner plate. He had literally collapsed into his mashed potato, face first! Everyone fell silent, and as we all sat staring, my best friend Trish came out onto the veranda for an impromptu visit. Frank raised his face from his plate; his rather pink, round face was splattered with mashed potato.

"He looks like Miss Piggy," Trish whispered, a bit too loud, and everyone burst out laughing...even Julie. Frank started snoring!

The next morning, when we all set out for a picnic day ride, Frank was very subdued. Steve brought the picnic lunch by car, with table and chairs for everyone's comfort. He would also bring swimming costumes / towels for anyone who wanted to swim in the river at the picnic location. He usually brought a bottle of wine, but after discussing it, we decided against it on this occasion, it would be easy to use the excuse that it was not good to ride a horse after drinking alcohol, and Frank looked as though he was nursing a massive hangover.

Later in the week, we had another problem with Frank and Harrie overtaking the other horses without warning, on a track that was not suitable for overtaking. The two girls Emma and Jayne were furious; Smartie, whose nickname was "little sports car," had tried to bolt after Harrie, really scaring Emma. Roxy had thrown a huge buck, almost unseating Jayne. This behaviour was out of character for Harrie, although he was a very fast horse, he had always been perfectly controllable; it was not like him to act like this, so I was pretty sure that Frank was instigating it. Then I had an idea.

Frank had said on a few occasions how beautiful Trovão was. Now, something I had noticed about Trovão was that although he looked big and powerful, he was really just a kitten. He had such a high stepping action that his stride didn't actually go very far, especially at canter. He didn't seem to have that racing urge that Thoroughbreds and Arabs have. He was wonderfully comfortable to ride, he felt like a rocking horse, but when you pushed him to go a little faster...nothing happened! I asked Frank if he would like to be the first guest to ride Trovão, and he said he would love to. My problems were over and our last two rides went without a hitch. Frank's drinking continued, but that wasn't my problem, as long as he was sober when riding!

CHAPTER 18

FARMYARD MASSACRE

As a particularly heavy shower slowly lumbered away, a thick heavily coloured rainbow seemed to slice down over our pastures. The bloated raindrops sparkled on the oily olive tree leaves, turning our field into a magical fairy grotto in the late afternoon sun. Then, as the sun slipped behind the clouds, the scene returned to normal...a muddy horse's field! We released the horses into the quagmire, and first one, then another crumpled down to roll; eventually the whole herd were gleefully plastering themselves in thick mud such as they had not seen for many a dry month.

Friends of ours had just bought an old farm about an hour's drive from us. We had originally met them when they came for a riding holiday at the same time as Crocodile Christine. Since then, they had been back for a couple more holidays before deciding to buy a property for their retirement here in Portugal. They were only in their forties, but were both prosperous, with money to spare. Although they were both business people, John yearned to be a farmer, he wanted to plough his own land, and grow his own crops. Penny was a lover of the Portuguese Lusitano horses, and wanted to train a Lusitano of her own to compete in dressage competitions. They had finally found their dream farm, and had invited us over to see it.

We had only planned to be away from our farm for three or four hours, and would be home to lock up the chicken/duck hotel before dark. The farm that the couple had found was a real gem. It was about four times the size of our house, but similar in structure with high ceilings and ancient wooden beams. It was like a huge banquet hall, but it had been neglected for many years and would need updating. Penny and John were keen to keep as many of the original features as possible; it would be a huge undertaking, and John would definitely need a tractor, as the land was also extensive, and out of control. Brambles reigned, it was impossible to walk around the land without being attacked by the barbed thorns, but John didn't seem to be deterred by all of the work, because after all, they had many years before they would be living there full time.

Penny and John invited us out for a meal to celebrate; Craig was away for the weekend so we couldn't call him to lock up the fowl hotel. We knew we should be on our way home, but how could we refuse? They were so excited. We had a lovely celebratory meal, not giving our ducks and chickens another thought—until we arrived home. It was a bloodbath. There were decapitated bodies littered everywhere as our car headlights illuminated the yard. I cried out in shock and horror, and wandered around the yard, a bit like a headless chicken myself.

"There's nothing we can do tonight," uttered Steve, sounding equally shocked. "Let's just check the 'hotel' to see if any managed to survive". It was empty.

Next morning, we steeled ourselves for clearing up the dead bodies. As I walked into the yard, I heard a distant sound of 'quack, quack', and looking over into the horse's field, I saw that Roxy, as usual, was standing as close to our house as he could possibly get, and standing underneath his belly, was a single duck. The lone survivor was one of the fully grown babies which had not been named because he was destined for the table. He came waddling towards me, under the electric fence, and I knelt down to pet him. He looked uninjured, and ate the grain that I held out for him. Over the next few weeks, he was named 'Fiery Fred, the fox fighting duck'; and he became a family pet. He refused to put one webbed foot inside the hotel, and instead took to sleeping next to or underneath Roxy. Roxy had never integrated within the herd of the other horses; he liked to be near them, but preferred to stay close to our house at night, so I always put his pile of hay apart from the other horses and close to our house. Roxy and Fred became inseparable, even when Roxy was in his stable, Fred hung around outside picking up any food that Roxy dropped; we cut a duck sized hole in Roxy's wooden door, and Fred would make himself a nest in one corner, so that he could sleep safely.

Steve was still going back to England to top up our bank account, not as frequently as he had at the beginning of our Portugal adventure, but it was still necessary occasionally. He was lucky that he had a friend in Brighton with a taxi; Steve had kept his taxi licence up to date, so he could just jump on a plane and step straight into a cab....to drive it, not as a passenger!

Steve wanted to build a conservatory onto our house, and he preferred to earn the money rather than try to take out a loan. He would be away for two whole months; I always dreaded him being away, but it was harder for him, he loved our farm and our way of life as much as I did, and the fact that he was willing to leave us and the farm behind, showed his commitment. He became miserable and depressed, and I had to prop him up with long phone calls telling him everything that was happening here. I didn't always feel able to support him because things were not good here.

Apollo was suffering with his third infection in his injured hoof. This meant that the vet had to be called, which in turn caused trauma for Apollo and anxiety to me. As soon as Apollo saw the vet's car coming down our drive, he became extremely agitated and uncontrollable; there was nothing I could do to console him. So far antibiotics had helped to clear up the infection, but the vet warned me, that this might not always be the case.

Francisco's new granddaughter was born, and within a few weeks he could be heard whistling his lullabies to the baby, while he worked in his field. Francisco was ageing; he seemed more hunched, making him appear even shorter than he was before! He still had a beautiful smile and a quick wit, along with plenty of village gossip to share with us. His wife Maria was ageing too. She had problems with her hips, and one morning as I was passing their house, Maria was waiting by her gate for a taxi to take her to hospital for an operation.

The local taxi firm arranged runs to Coimbra hospital almost daily. It was their 'bread and butter'. The driver would pick up anyone in the area with a hospital appointment, often up to four people, and take them into Coimbra which was a 45 minute ride; then he would wait all day for those that were coming back home. The cost was shared which made it affordable even for poor mountain folk, and the whole experience was so much more enjoyable for them than a long slow infrequent bus journey. I wished her well, as she painfully climbed into the taxi, but she was soon chatting away to two other ladies who were already in the cab.

Paul, my son was coming for a holiday. Sadly, he had broken up with Natalie, although I had heard from a friend of theirs that things hadn't been good between them for a while, so the news hadn't come as a complete surprise. I must admit that I was looking forward of having both of my sons all to myself for a week.

Craig and I had a lovely week with Paul, visiting all the local swimming spots. I was more than happy to just swim in the river below our house, but this area has so many beautiful river spots that whenever we had family or friends staying with us, we did try to make an effort to visit other places. Góis has a wonderful swimming river, you can swim upstream in deep clear water, completely surrounded by nature, and this is where we chose to swim on the first day of his holiday.

Ancient trees hung over the river, their large tangled roots clinging to the steep bank reminded me of an old witch's gnarled hand. The roots were becoming more exposed each year as the winter rains washed away the soil. As we swam, we imagined what animals had made their homes in the burrows and holes along the river bank—otters and voles for sure, and as we were talking I heard the familiar shrill sound of an approaching kingfisher. We waited in anticipation, and in the blink of an eye, it flew past us and our eyes were only just able to register its bright blue plumage zooming past, almost touching the water like a missile. A snake was lazily swimming up river from us; I'd say it was a big one by the size of its head, held above the water, and by the ripples which were slowly spreading out over the surface of the river.

"Come on, I think it's time to go back for an ice cream", I whispered as I turned away from the seemingly oblivious creature.

Craig was waiting for us at the river's edge; he was sitting with a group of friends, but jumped up as we approached, and came with us to sit at the outdoor cafe on the bank of the river. Sometimes the temperature can reach 40 degrees, and the café owner would put his tables and chairs in a shallow part of the river. We all sat with our feet in the cool water, and ordered a 'cachorro' which is a hot dog, served with mustard, tomato sauce and mayonnaise and topped with copiously sprinkled potato sticks. It's deliciously messy to eat. We washed it down with a cold panaché, which is a shandy, so good on a hot day!

Another day, we drove further up the mountain to a river beach nourished by a waterfall. There was a cave that you could crawl through, which came out under the waterfall. The boys crawled through the cave and dived into the cascading water. I was content to watch and guard our picnic! We also visited Cabreira, which is a charming village, high in the mountains. The villagers used to store their olives in little stone huts, situated close to the olive pressing shed, on the banks of the river. It's all in ruins now, and these days the little stone huts are mainly used as changing rooms as it's a popular bathing area for locals and holidaymakers. There was no cafe there, so we strolled back into town for lunch after an eye-wateringly refreshing swim...the water this far up the mountain is freezing even in summer.

Paul told us that he had a new girlfriend, and he was happy in his job and in his life, which is all, as a mother, I could ask for. Paul is an Anglophile, particularly for the Brighton area where he had been born. I wouldn't be surprised if he lived in the area all of his life. Mella was different; she loved Portugal, and was restless in England. She and Simon were already making plans to move out here in the future.

As I was waving goodbye to Paul, I saw the taxi pull up outside Francisco's house, and the driver helped Maria out of the passenger seat. Francisco came out to meet her, and the two of them went slowly into their little house. Their daughter arrived; she was very good to them, and I knew she would look after her mother better than anyone else could.

During July and August there are some big festivals in the sleepy town of Góis. In July, there is an art show, which has been growing year by year, with more artists bringing their paintings, sculptures and ceramic work to display. The week finishes with a fantastic fireworks display.

Steve had only arrived back from England that afternoon, and although he was tired, he wanted to go and watch the spectacle. As usual in Portugal, the evening was running late and it was midnight before the show started. We were with a group of friends, who were all getting a bit frustrated and tired, when we heard in the distance the sound of music coming from up river. The complex, sweet sound drifted closer in the dark night sky, until we could see a boat aflame with lights, and the silhouette of a solitary man, with a saxophone to his lips, sailing down the river towards us. It was just magical. Then without warning, there was an explosion of light and sound, as hundreds of fireworks lit up the night sky. It was spectacular, but the mystical mellow sound of the saxophone drifting in the star-studded sky was what had truly enchanted me.

During August, we visited the Góis authentic festival, where there were displays of the arts and crafts of the area. A lady sat on a three-legged stool, spinning wool from her herd of sheep, on an antique spinning wheel. Mountain folk brought their artisan olive oil, honey, dried cherries, and also various fruit-based alcohols to sell on stalls that had been set up for the occasion. There were children's fairground rides, and hot dog/candyfloss vans competing with Fartura vans, which is the Portuguese equivalent of doughnuts, sprinkled with cinnamon and lots of sugar: very yummy.

An old man from a village near us put on a display of how things worked in olden times. Over the years, he had built miniature authentic working water wheels, where water spilled from tiny wooden cups; he had also built models of flint water mills with working stone wheels that turned as the water gushed through them. He set up on trestle tables next to a weir, and using an open topped plastic pipe, he channelled water from the river into the pipe; this flow of water set his water wheels and mills into action, demonstrating how people had depended on the river in the olden days. It amazed me how many children and young people were interested in watching and learning from him, as he told how their grandparents and great-grandparents had lived. To these youngsters, the river was a place for cooling off and having fun on hot days, not for grinding maize and producing olive oil.

Most of the larger villages had a brass band; in Portuguese it is called the Filarmónica. Our local village of Vila Nova do Ceira has a very good band, called Filvar. Recently they had been practising constantly in the church hall, and when we were shopping in the local supermarket, or even just walking around the village, we could hear them playing. They would be strong contenders in the competition, which would be played out in heats each evening all through the festival. They were a dedicated band, encouraging a lot of young musicians, and we were hoping that they would be the winners of the coveted cup.

As this authentic festival drew to a close, Góis had another spectacle starting. It was a motor bike festival. It started in 1991, when a group of friends got together to ride in the mountains during their summer holidays. By the late 90s, it had grown hugely; hundreds of bikers descended on the little town to ride bikes, talk bikes, and party!

Makeshift cafes and bars appeared along the river bank to accommodate the growing crowds, and bands were organised to play pop and rock music into the early hours. It was great fun in those early days, when anyone could wander through the park. My friend Trish and I loved to wander along the riverbank which was lined with some fantastic vintage and brand-new motorbikes. There were lavish American chopper style bikes painted in gold, parked next to old 1960s Lambretta scooters...and everything in between. At nightfall we would dance to some great tribute bands and drink too many margaritas!

In the daytime, the bikes and their riders would parade around the streets and mountain roads. Helmets seemed to be off limits, and so did sensible bike attire. There were plenty of bikini clad pillion passengers, hanging on to tattooed, muscle bound men, wearing unzipped leather waistcoats. We also heard a much higher volume of ambulance sirens that week than usual...ouch!

As the years went by and the festival grew, bigger 'named' rock bands were booked, fences were erected, a campsite was set up, and nobody could enter the now enclosed park without buying a ticket, which became more expensive each year. Yes, progress, I know, but I still yearn for the old days, when I could freely wander along the river bank with a bag of sugary farturas, listening to local bands and having fun. I remember one year there was a Portuguese Bob Marley tribute band playing; they were absolutely fabulous, playing all of the old hits, and getting everyone dancing in the street.

CHAPTER 19

THE SPIRIT OF THE RIVER RAN THROUGH ME

The summer festivals gave way to the quiet of autumn. The river bank park in the centre of town which had been a lively, noisy place of rock bands and summer fun was now shrouded in falling leaves from the ancient trees which had shaded the picnic tables throughout the summer. Just the occasional lonely person strolled through the leaf litter; the swings in the children's park were all empty, and the river was roaring after a recent storm.

Our farm was about 5k downriver, and on such days, when the river was high, I loved to immerse myself in it. Not to swim, it was too fierce and cold now, but just to sit and allow it to flow through my mind, cleansing my thoughts.

The winter months are when the otters breed, and I had heard them calling to one another earlier; I wasn't sure if the teenage pups had become separated from their mother in the storm, or if it were a male and female calling to each other. I made myself comfortable on the bank, and wondered what I might see. Even though I sat watching and waiting, I was still surprised when from the middle of the fast-flowing river, two large adult otters rose up together, and it looked as if they were fighting. I was mesmerised. They dived underwater, and surfaced again and again; I was sure they were fighting and not mating. They were both totally oblivious of me sitting quietly on the bank. They looked well matched, and neither was giving way. I was so engrossed that I didn't even pick up my camera and take a photo or a video; it just didn't occur to me. After what seemed like about 10 minutes, one otter didn't resurface, and my heart lurched. Then I saw him swim over the weir, and disappear from sight. He had been vanquished, and I assumed that the victorious male would be the father of next year's young.

A murder of crows was cawing in the high trees; they were aware of my presence, and were restless to roost for the night. A chill breeze had picked up, so I stiffly rose from my viewing platform, and left the river bank to the animals.

Mr Piggy (I know that's cruel, but I can't help myself!) and his long-suffering wife Julie, requested to book another holiday for the next year. I didn't know what to think, but as Steve pointed out, we couldn't really afford to turn people away. I convinced myself, that they had been good riders, they just liked a bit of speed, which I was rather partial to myself! As long as I didn't book anyone else in for the week that they were coming, what could go wrong? I had changed the wording on the website from 'As much wine as you can drink', to a more conservative 'Wine/beer/soft drinks, served with meals.' I just hoped that they would re-read the website before their arrival.

The lovely family that had helped us build our arena, were also coming back during the summer holidays, and I had booked another family in for the same week, with a young daughter of the same age as Sandy, so hopefully that would work out well. It was always nice to see the bookings starting to come in, it helped me peep out from my perpetual cloud of doubt, fearing that nobody would come.

The first group of the year were three Danish riders. Now I always imagine Danes to be tall and blonde, so I was quite taken aback when three very short, stocky people arrived, two men and one woman; all with beards, long hair and smoking pipes! The group consisted of husband and wife and the wife's father. I can't remember their names, but the father was a real character. All three were obsessive about Icelandic horses, and were rather derogatory when I introduced them to my horses. When I took them to see Harrie; saying that one of them would be riding him for the week, they scoffed and said "No horse needs to be that big." I was truly offended: Harrie was a fantastic horse. They gave similar 'compliments' to all the other horses, until the father stopped at Roxy and said.

"This one will do for me."

Icelandic horses are a tough small breed, capable of withstanding Icelandic conditions, but they wouldn't thrive in the hot summers of Portugal. I couldn't understand why this family had booked a riding holiday in Southern Europe, yet they expected to ride Icelandic horses. It didn't make sense; our website gave a detailed description of all of our horses and lots of pictures too. The daughter chose Comet, who was small and stocky, and her husband 'relented' to ride my gorgeous Lusitano x Thoroughbred, Harrie.

After a few drinks, the evenings didn't go too badly, the father loved to tell tales of all his adventures, and he'd had quite a few! They all sat puffing on their pipes; I didn't dare tell them that we had a no smoking policy! The father always insisted on wearing a full length waxed coat when riding. He always got too hot and had to hang it across the saddle. One day while out riding, he was in the middle of one of his tales, when he realised that the coat had gone, it must have slipped off, probably as we were crossing a river where the horses had to jump out of the water onto a steep bank, which they always trotted up to give them more traction. Roxy always enjoyed this manoeuvre, and would canter up the steep bank, probably causing the coat to slip off. When we got home, Steve offered to go and look for the coat on his motor bike, but it was never found.

When Frank (Mr Piggy) and Julie arrived a few weeks later, Steve and I were both amazed: we hardly recognised Frank. He had lost weight; his face was no longer quite so round, and his cheeks had lost the pink puffiness; he actually looked great. He noticed our surprised faces, and in his old cocky way said.

"What do you think of the new me? It's all down to Julie," he added as he put an arm around her. Later, over dinner Frank explained.

"She threatened to leave me if I didn't change my ways, but I didn't believe her, so she left. I was devastated, but it forced me to face up the fact that I was a compulsive drinker, and I couldn't stop. Julie encouraged me to reach out for professional help, and that was a game changer."

"Things are better than they have been for years," quipped Julie, smiling and taking Frank's hand. "And we have been taking jumping lessons and are thinking about buying ourselves a horse each and maybe even competing. You don't want to sell Guv, do you?"

"Guv's competing days are over," I laughed, "He's 20 years old this year, but you are welcome to ride him for this week".

We had a very nice week in their company, and would have welcomed them back, but as Julie said, once they bought two horses, holidays would be a thing of the past!

Apollo had yet another infection in his hoof. I could tell he was in pain as he wouldn't put any weight on it at all, which meant that he was standing crooked and putting strain on his back as well as his other legs. My vet, Diogo, had warned me last time that if it happened again, I should really think about having him euthanized. At the time, I couldn't even think about it, Apollo was too precious, I loved him too much. But over time I had conceded that I must put my own emotions aside. This awful situation was never going to get better, and each time he caught an infection, it seemed to be worse; yet he was only 9 years old, still a baby—how could I find the strength to do as the vet said?

Steve made the call; I just couldn't do it. Diogo asked Steve to try to make sure that I wasn't present. Apollo was very resistant to vets and he thought it would be dangerous to have the two of us in the stable while he was administering the lethal drug. But how could I just leave him? I should be there, by his side. Diogo arrived, and told me that he would give Apollo a small injection to calm him first. I insisted on standing at his head and covering his eye so that he couldn't see the needle, as I had always done, and Diogo agreed. Apollo was much more frightened than usual, probably because of his pain, and he surged forward, crushing my ribs against the stable door, as the injection hit home.

It wasn't long before drowsiness overcame him, and I opened the door and limped away; my ribs throbbed, but with the anguish in my heart, I didn't feel anything. Diogo was loading the big vial, he told me that Apollo wouldn't know if I was there or not, and he would prefer it if I left. Steve led me away, but I pulled away from him and ran to the river.

And the spirit of the river ran through me, allowing my tears to add to its torrent, blocking all noise except for its continuous roar. The white water gushed over the weir, spraying my salty wet face with cool, clean water: and I felt calm, I knew he was at peace.

I would not be allowed to bury Apollo on our farm as we were too close to the river and leaking body fluids could contaminate the water table. I had to wait three days until a truck was sent from a council yard to pick up the stiff body, which was dragged from the stable by a pulley, and lifted by a small crane mounted on the truck. I didn't watch, but I heard the sounds of the engine and men's voices shouting orders. Then he was gone.

CHAPTER 20

GOLEGÃ

A mother and her two daughters were staying with us for a riding holiday. One morning, the youngest girl, called Stacey, shyly told me that she had heard meowing and when she followed the sound, she found three little kittens. It had become a familiar story to us, but to her it was magical. Two of the kittens had vanished into the undergrowth, but the third one had timidly followed her, and lapped up a saucer of milk.

Taming the kittens became her quest and she spent all of her free time with them. The first one was a very pretty little ginger kitten that she called Lion King. He was her favourite and she was soon able to pick him up and cuddle him. She begged her mother to be allowed to take him home, and eventually her mother relented. He would have to wait until he had been to the vet and had his vaccinations and passport sorted out, but after that they would arrange for a pet transport company to deliver him to their home in England.

So, then there were two, one male and one female. We already had two male cats, and they made it very clear that they would not accept another male, although they were happy to welcome the little female! Craig had a friend, whose parents were looking for a kitten, so they came and took the male tabby. The little black female was my favourite. She was half the size of her brothers, really petite and very cuddly and I was happy for her to stay. I called her Kitty.

We were expecting some guests that had been many times before. Gill and Colin had been here on the day that Domino arrived at our farm, they were definitely some of our favourite guests, good riders and great fun. Gill was the biggest cat lover in the world, and I knew she was going to love our new little Kitty. Steve had just gone to pick them up from the airport for another holiday; I had stayed at home to muck out the stables and was just taking a full wheelbarrow of poo around to the muckheap, when I was stopped in my tracks by a noise. It was raining and quite cold, I could hear a definite crying whimpering sound, and looking around me I saw a movement close to the muckheap.

It was a little brown creature, and my first impression was that it was a wild baby pig; I strained my eyes and ears thinking that the mother could be close by, but as I edged closer, I realised that it was a tiny puppy. It was soaking wet and covered in mud, and as I picked him up, his little damp body, snuggled into my warmth. His eyes still had a hint of blue, but I thought he could see around him, so he was probably about a month old. He looked quizzically up into my face; it was the cutest little face I had ever seen; I cuddled him closer, and took him indoors.

I had some leftover chicken from last night's dinner, which I chopped up and offered to him. He ate ravenously, as though he had never seen food before: maybe he had only had his mother's milk. I took the bowl away from him so that he could not gorge himself; if his tummy wasn't used to solid food, it could upset his digestion. He was lapping up some water when Craig came into the kitchen with Moppy and Bica. They were both curious and wanted to sniff him; the little mite cowered and tucked his tail between his legs, but he accepted their scrutiny.

Moppy, who only weighed 4 kilos, towered over him, she bossily tried to push him away from the water bowl; she had never had anything to boss before but I had a feeling that she wouldn't be bossing this little guy for long. He had quite big paws, and I was sure he would grow much bigger than our little Mop. Craig bent down to stroke him, and his hand came away with a stripe of mud across his palm.

"He needs a bath!" he exclaimed, going to the sink to wash his hands. We ran a bowl of warm soapy water, and gently lowered him into it. His cute little eyes never left my face as I reassured him, but his body quaked in fear. We bathed him as quickly as possible, and wrapped him in a big warm towel. With all the mud washed off, we could now see that he was tri coloured. He had a white chest which continued around his neck and under his belly, his little head and ears were brown, as were his back and tail, he had a black splodge in the middle of his back, which almost looked as though he was wearing a saddle!

I had just managed to dry him, when I heard our car come rumbling down our cobbled driveway. Steve was back from the airport with Colin and Gill. I tucked the now fluffy little puppy into my sweatshirt, and pulling up the zip, I ran outside to greet them. I laughed at their curious faces as I stood there with a lump in my tummy, Steve laughed too, thinking I had tucked our new little kitten into my sweatshirt to surprise Gill. Steve's face changed from laughter to shock as I lowered my zip, and a little brown puppy head popped out! Steve's face fell, and I could see him mouthing the words "Oh, no."

Gill picked up little Kitty, who was already winding herself around her legs.

"Oh, what a little sweetie," purred Gill, "you realise that you won't be seeing much of her this week don't you; she is coming to live with me in the cottage! The little pup is cute too, what is his name?"

"I only found him an hour ago...give me a chance!" I chastised. At that moment, Craig ran down the steps.

"His name is Scratch" he said, as he hugged Colin and Gill. "I was listening to a reggae artist called Lee Scratch Perry, when Mum brought him home, so I think it's an appropriate name. It suits him, look at his scratchy little face," he said as he took him from my arms. "I think he will be living with me: my little reggae boy." And from then until Craig left home, Scratch slept on his bed.

We never found out where he came from, but it's possible that he may have been from a litter of a stray female dog. Every village had an old lady that would feed stray dogs and cats, and a few weeks later, we saw a stray dog with two pups, and one of them looked a bit like Scratch; they all bolted for the hills when they saw us. I wonder what fate held in store for them?

"You should have called him Lucky!" Steve quipped.

Little Kitty was not so lucky though. When she was 5 months old, I took her to the vet to have her sterilised. She had hardly grown at all and she had lumps under her stomach, which on an earlier visit, the vet had said were probably just fatty lumps. However, once he prepared her for the operation, he realised that she was riddled with cancer and after phoning us with the sad news, he put her to sleep. The two boy kittens grew strong and healthy, and little Stacey still sends me pictures of Lion King.

In early November, the local villages celebrate Magusto—the chestnut harvest. Small fires are lit in village squares, and sometimes people jump over the flames just for fun. The sulphurous smell of singed hair from the men's hairy legs as they leap over the flames is quite repugnant, but once the flames die down, children throw chestnuts that they have collected from the forest into the fire to roast. Jeropega is a very sweet strong wine made from a mix of grape juice and aguardente, which is a Portuguese type of brandy. The sweet taste of Jeropega goes very well with the starchy taste of the chestnuts. It is drunk in copious amounts at these festivals, which can become very rowdy, with accordion music and dancing through the dusty ashes.

November is also the time of the biggest horse fair in Portugal, in a town called Golegã, which is in the Alentejo region. This year our riding guests had asked if we could include a day out at Golegã as part of their riding week. I was very happy to oblige as I loved the whole atmosphere and spirit of the festival. It is truly a celebration of the Lusitano horse; well worth a visit for anyone who loves horses. I have visited many horse festivals and shows but have never witnessed anything like Golegã. The atmosphere is electric as the festival takes over the normally quiet streets of the whole town.

Magnificent Lusitanos are all around you, being ridden through the narrow streets four abreast; the riders in their formal black and grey livery expect you to move out of the way. If you manage to dodge them, then listen out for the tinkling bells on the colourful carriages drawn by two or four horses that can be seen trotting around the streets full of tourists. There is a fairground, and Portuguese music blaring from the many newly erected bars and stalls.

The main arena is for show jumping and dressage competitions, which are held throughout the day and night. There are also carriage driving competitions and working equitation competitions, where the rider has to steer his/her horse around obstacles that could be met in a working environment. These manoeuvres would include opening a gate on horseback, tackling small jumps, and weaving through obstacles. It is a test of the horse's agility and ability to listen to the rider's instructions.

There are horses for sale, as well as saddles and all types of leatherwear, from boots to handbags. Ginjinha bars are set up at every corner, selling tiny chocolate cups filled with Ginja, a sweet cherry liqueur that the Portuguese love. Oh, it is so nice! The wafts of smoke from the chestnut sellers fill the air as they constantly roast chestnuts which they serve in paper cones: very hard to resist.

All around this huge competition arena is a sand track. It is about 15 metres wide and half a kilometre in circumference. Stunning stallions and their riders parade around the track. Sometimes there can be 100 horses, mostly stallions, parading at the same time. I love to stand on the fence line and watch the parading horses, they are just so beautiful. I had met an old friend at the fair and we stood together for a while. She was watching the handsome Portuguese riders and whispered to me, "Oh, he is nice," as four horses and riders came towards us, but I was too busy watching the horses to notice a mere human! At that moment all four stopped trotting and started doing the dressage movement piaffe, which is performed by the horse springing energetically from one diagonal pair of legs to the other, yet not moving forward. It was horse ballet at its best. And of course the handsome and skilled Portuguese riders, added to the overall spectacle!

While these wonderful horses were performing high quality dressage, two young boys on scraggly ponies came galloping around the arena, seemingly out of control. No one shouted at them or seemed angry, everyone was in high spirits, and the four dressage riders totally ignored them, as did everyone else.

There were gaps in the fencing so that people could cross the sand track and watch the competitions taking place in the arena. There were no safety gates or marshals controlling the crowds, people just wandered across in front of the riders on the track! Everyone seemed so chilled and happy in the warm November

173

sunshine. We all had to stop at a hat stall and buy sunhats, it was so hot!

As evening drew in, the blue sky was streaked with pink and red as the sun sunk for another day. The smells of barbecue filled the air, as cafes and restaurants around the perimeter of the sand track, began to fill with hungry diners. We found a table for our group of four; oh, it was such a relief to sit down, yet I didn't want to miss anything. We still hadn't visited all of the stalls, so after a huge slap-up meal, we all set out into the brightly lit up night to spend some money!

I bought a very ornate bridle which was black leather with lots of brass bling; it would look stunning on Trovão and the stall-holder who sold it to me also threw in a pair of matching reins just because he was in such a good mood...although he was drinking red wine from a pint glass at the time; also his extravagant body language and booming voice, telling everyone around that he was giving away free reins, certainly brought a crowd to his stall.

One of our guests bought a really stylish, handmade leather wide-brimmed hat, and our other guest bought a beautiful hand-bag, and an ornate belt to take home for her boyfriend. We all called into a street bar for a beer, and couldn't believe our eyes when two riders rode their horses straight into the bar and ordered wine right next to us! Another man was sitting on his horse in the bar, he was talking on his phone and smoking a cigarette whilst his horse performed perfect piaffe ...Incredible!

I could have stayed all night, the festival didn't seem to be slowing down; in fact, I think the throngs of people were denser than earlier, there was a big show jumping finale about to start in the main arena, and the sand track was still pounding with the rhythmical beat of hundreds of hooves. The exuberant crowd would be partying all night long; but we had a long drive home, and we were all tired. Tomorrow I had planned our 'Top of the world' picnic ride, which meant an early start. It was a long ride but would be our last of the season; we had managed to rent a big field where the horses would spend the next three months just being free.

CHAPTER 21

A NEW BEGINNING

Mella and Simon had been to stay for a holiday in September; they had seemed more blissfully happy than ever before and would disappear down by the river for hours. So when I had a phone call from them, I half expected them to tell me that they were getting married. But I was elated by what she told me...I was going to be a grandmother. They were coming out to us for Christmas so I would have to wait until then to give them both a big hug. I was so excited that I didn't know how I could wait until the day the baby was born. I could remember feeling the same way with my own pregnancies; it was such a long wait to meet the new little life that was growing inside of me. It really is one of the wonders of the world.

In May 2009, my first grandchild was born. A little girl called Maia. I flew to England to meet her. I had forgotten the wonderful smell of a newborn, the softness of her head, and the endearing little mewling noises as she hungrily sucked her own fist. Maia was absolutely delightful, and we planned a family party to celebrate her birth. It was a warm spring day, and my mother had been busy making finger food that we could eat out on her lawn. Maia was her first great-grandchild, and we took a photo of the four generations. My mum hardly looked old enough to be a grandmother, let alone a great-grandmother. She really did look very young for her age. I hope I have her youth gene!

Before Mella's pregnancy, she had been riding a friend's horse called Joey. He was a bit of a nutcase and reminded me of a young

Roxy. His owner wanted to sell him and Mella was keen to buy him. She and Simon were still talking about moving to Portugal and she wanted to bring Joey with her. She thought he would be great for experienced riders who wanted a challenge and I agreed. I really needed a new challenge to help mend the massive hole left by Apollo; I missed him so much, but maybe Joey could be the horse to heal me. We started to plan for his arrival in Portugal.

Mella's other horse called Ucarius,(aka Teddy Bear) had navicular, a lameness of the hoof; he would never be sound enough for serious work, but liked to go out for walks when he was feeling good. An older lady had been helping Mella look after him throughout her pregnancy, and the lady asked Mella if she could move Ucarius closer to her own home so that she could look after him for the rest of his life. This lady loved him, and would take good care of him, so Mella sadly agreed and said goodbye to her big Teddy Bear.

As soon as she was fit enough after the birth, Mella was up at the stables riding Joey in the arena while Maia slept in her pram. Maia was around horses from day one, and as soon as she could sit up, she was sitting on a horse: right from the start, it was her happy place

Joey arrived in Portugal the following spring, I really enjoyed riding him and so did some of our experienced guests, but as time went on, he became more uncontrollable, and I always had a nagging feeling that he wasn't happy here. Mella, Simon and Maia finally moved to Portugal with their springer spaniel Ray in September. They brought my mum out with them for a holiday, and we all had a lovely two weeks together. When my mum returned to England, we started to prepare for our next guests.

We were fully booked for October, and Mella was keen to help. We had a few regular riders who lived locally, Bess had been riding with me for a year or so, and another nice girl called Carla also came at the same time. They usually shared a lesson, but sometimes they liked to hack out in the mountains. Mella had qualified as a riding teacher, so she took over all of the school work. She rode Joey out in the mountains whenever she could, but like me, she began to think that he was not happy.

My horses did have to spend a lot of time in their stables, summer grazing was non-existent, and as the sun and flies got too much for them; they would come and stand in their cool stables by choice, but Joey was different. He hated his stable, and the only way to get him through the door was by bribing him with a bucket of food. He had lived in a big green field all year round in the south of England. He was becoming frustrated with life in Portugal and riding him was becoming quite dangerous. One time while I was riding him up a steep hill, his rein broke at the point where it affixes to the bit. I had to jump off and fix it with a bit of string that I always carried in my pocket, but then I had to get back on to this crazy horse that had no intention of standing still for me. I put one foot in the stirrup and leapt up, just as he took off at a flat-out gallop. Somehow I pulled myself across the saddle, I felt like a Cossack stunt rider!

On the way home from our rides, there was a lovely track that was slightly uphill and nice and wide. It wound gently around the hillside, and all the horses loved to canter homeward bound. Before we reached this track however, there was a steep downhill rocky track that needed to be negotiated slowly and carefully, but Joey had different ideas. He would leap up into the air, and try his hardest to pull the reins from my hands so that he could gallop down the hill and beat all of the other horses home. He was becoming a danger not only to himself, but to me and the other horses and riders.

When Mella had lived in England, she had ridden with a young lad who specialised in re-training horses. He knew Joey well, and was sure that if we sent him back to England, he could re-train him and find him a good home with not a stable in sight! He kept his word and found the very best home for Joey. The girl that bought him still keeps in touch with us and adores him.

We had a Portuguese friend who owned a goat farm quite near to us. He asked Steve if he could hire our horsebox to move his goats as he was selling them, and needed to transport them to their new home. He had 40 goats of all different sizes, Steve didn't see how they could all fit into our horsebox, but Gonçalo assured him that it would be possible. So, a few days later, Gonçalo herded all 40 goats into our horsebox, and Steve drove them with Gonçalo as a passenger, to their new home. All went well, but what we hadn't thought about was the mess and smell made by 40 frightened goats! Our horsebox still had a lingering smell of goat many months later, despite numerous attempts to fumigate it.

Gonçalo's next venture was to be a chicken farmer. He wanted Steve to go into business with him. Thankfully Steve wasn't keen on the idea, and Gonçalo didn't go ahead with that venture. He was a bit of an entrepreneur and had noticed that more and more foreigners were coming to this area looking for real estate. His next business plan was to set himself up as a real estate agent.

There were very few agents in this area that specialised in selling old forgotten plots of land and ruins. Portuguese people hadn't woken up to the fact yet, that an old shack on a piece of land that their granddad grew corn on or kept his goats in, had any value at all. The younger generation had busy city lives, and the old house that their grandparents used to farm in bygone days was of no monetary significance to them. Henceforth there were many old neglected ruins and overgrown land plots that people thought were worthless. Gonçalo had lived in the area all of his life, and knew just about everyone. He talked to people in local bars and offered to buy these worthless plots; then he would sell them on at a tidy profit to foreigners who were looking to escape city life, and were enthralled by the idea of a small retreat in the Portuguese mountains. He employed a team of workers to renovate these old hidden gems, and before long, he had many Portuguese people asking him to buy their old rustic plots. And on the other side of the coin, through word of mouth, and of course the internet, foreigners were coming to him to help them search for their dream retreat in the Portuguese mountains.

One day, Gonçalo came to ask me if I could teach him to ride. He had decided that he wanted to buy a horse. I was happy to give him lessons, and tried to impart some knowledge of horse care into the sessions. He was very confident, and on my faithful Guv he learnt quickly, but after only half a dozen lessons, he arrived one day to tell me that he had bought a horse. He loved Trovao, my black Lusitano, and proudly showed me photographs on his phone of a black Lusitano horse. I was taken aback when he told me that the horse was only four years old, he was so excited that I didn't want to dampen his enthusiasm, but a very novice rider with a very young horse is not a good combination.

While Steve was away working in England, Gonçalo started coming around to our house, inviting me out to dinner and making me feel uncomfortable. Eventually I had to be blunt with him, and tell him that I didn't want him coming to my home any more, and although I was interested in how he was getting on with his horse, and wanted to stay in touch with him, I was not interested in any-thing else. I didn't see him again for over 6 months.

Next time Gonçalo came to the house, Steve was home so I was happy to invite him in, and I asked him how he was getting on with his horse. He told us that the horse was turned out in a large field alone, with no companions, and was becoming wild. He blamed everything on the horse...the horse was bad, he told me, it had thrown him off many times and he wanted to sell it.

I could picture the scenario differently. He was a big strong in-experienced rider, trying to ride a very young horse. He told us that every time he mounted and tried to make the horse move forward, it reared and threw him off. I could imagine him taking the reins up much too short, and hauling himself up into the saddle, which would undoubtedly unbalance a young horse, and combined with the fact that Gonçalo was using a very strong bit in the poor young horse's soft mouth, and pulling too hard on the reins, the horse had no option but to rear in pain and fear. I felt sorry for the horse...not the rider!

Gonçalo asked me if he could bring the horse to my farm as he had to go away for six months. He would pay for its costs, and if I managed to sell the horse, he would give me a percentage. I had a spare stable, so I agreed, and Ariano arrived at our farm a few days later to a rapturous welcome from our inquisitive neighing horses.

As the ramp of the horsebox was lowered, we caught our first glimpse of him. His hindquarters were visibly shaking as Mella slowly walked into the horsebox and gently stroked his face. It was as if she instinctively knew that there was something in this nerv-ous young horse that needed her. He had the most beautiful face but his eyes looked permanently worried. He was a very dark bay, almost black with no white markings at all. She led him into a sta-ble; she still hadn't said a word, then I heard her say,

"Shhh, you're home now" and as she stood stroking him, his tense body relaxed and their bond, which lasted until the day he died, was already formed.

Living alone in a large open space, as he had been, is not natural for a herd animal. Horses are prey animals and need the protection of a herd to feel safe. Now surrounded by other horses, he was much more relaxed, and as we got to know him we realised that he loved being in his stable. He was happy to be out in a paddock with other horses, but he hated to be alone.

We went back to basics with his training and took things slowly. He was becoming more confident, but if the slightest thing went wrong, he would threaten to rear, although he never actually did. I asked my vet to call and check his back and teeth. He told us that he knew Gonçalo and Ariano, and agreed that the problem was with Gonçalo and not Ariano. He found some very sharp teeth that were cutting into his lower gums causing him to have persistent ulcers in his mouth. His teeth were not well aligned so this would always be a problem for him and we would need to have his teeth checked every six months. The vet said that in his opinion, Ariano was a very nice horse that had been abused in his young life through ignorance more than cruelty. He said that Gonçalo would be better to buy a motor bike than another horse, and we agreed!

Mella bought Ariano from Gonçalo, and within a year he had taken over from Guv as our main lead horse. He was amazing, and when I rode him at the front of a trek, I really felt that he was totally tuned in to me: he trusted me and I trusted him, it was a wonderful relationship. His gallop was magical, I felt as though I was floating as his muscles moved under me, his long mane licking my face; yet even then he was listening to me, and when I asked him to slow down, his ear would flick backward, and he would begrudgingly slow his speed. He really was one of the most remarkable horses I had ever ridden. Mella and I, and later on Maia too, felt blessed to have him in our lives.

Scratchy, our little rescued pup, was now full grown and loved to come with us on our hacks. He would trot along beside me and Ariano at the front of a ride, and when we all wanted to canter, I would say "Down" to him, and he would sink down on the edge of the path so that all of the horses could canter past him; then he would run along behind us. He was a lovely dog, full of spirit and happiness. Craig had done some agility training with him; he had built a see-saw in the yard that Scratchy had to run up one side of, stop on the top, and then run down the other side. Craig had used some of my plastic electric fence posts to teach him to bend in and out of poles, and Scratch loved to jump over horse jumps in our arena. It was a shame that dog agility competitions were not popular at that time, as I'm sure he could have won!

Mella had brought her lovely dog called Ray with her from England, he was a brown and white springer spaniel, he was so gentle with Maia and used to sit under her high-chair and wait for her to drop little morsels of food! He thought he had moved to heaven when he saw our orange tree full of big round orange balls!

Paul, my eldest son, had a new girlfriend. Her name was Sarah, and she worked with him as a park ranger. He told us that they had a lot in common, especially their love of wildlife conservation, to which they were both totally committed. I could tell that he was captivated by her and I couldn't wait to meet her; I had already booked a flight to England to visit my family, so I wouldn't have long to wait.

I liked Sarah from the first moment I met her, she had lived in the south of England all of her life and loved the area, as did Paul. They fitted together perfectly as a couple and I had a strong feeling that he had found his lifetime partner. His job was going really well, he was being given a lot of scope to study the wildlife of the area. It was at a time of an awakening need for local councils to step up to the conservation challenge, and Paul had plenty of enthusiasm to teach and share his knowledge with as many of the general public as possible.

He was rewarded by being given the opportunity to manage the rewilding of an ancient Neolithic site of fragile chalk downland on the eastern side of Brighton, which was believed to have been inhabited 5500 years ago, but now it was covered in bushes and scrub that had crept slowly over the grassland. Most of the bushes and scrub would need to be cleared to improve light and growing conditions that would enable the old flora and fauna to re-establish itself. Once the wildflowers were growing again, they would attract rare chalk loving butterflies, bees and birds which had been declining for many years.

The grass would be grazed by sheep and wild ponies. My son was to become a shepherd! A local farmer would lease his sheep to the project for a few months a year to graze the land and Paul and a group of volunteers would keep an eye on them. Wild ponies would be released and allowed to live naturally. The public were encouraged to use the land but asked to keep to the paths. It was a huge project which Paul met with his usual passion and dedication.

Two years later, I was given the most wonderful news. I was to become a grandmother for the second time. Sarah gave birth to a baby boy. I booked my ticket to England and met my new little grandson Indi. All babies are beautiful, but your own are always a little more perfect and Indi was no exception; he was adorable, with huge blue eyes and long dark lashes. When he was a few months old, an old man stopped to admire him as he lay in his pram. Sarah was used to ladies stopping to coo at him, but it was not so normal for a man. He gently placed his palm on top of Indie's little hands, and said to Sarah.

"That boy has the sea in his eyes." This really resonated with me as my family on my father's side, had been lifeboat men since the 1800's.

Meanwhile back at the farm in Portugal, our Portuguese Water Dog Max was ailing. He had been an old dog when we had found him and we thought he was about 14 years old. He had always been in good health, just a little stiff in his joints, but one day as I put his bowl of food down for him, he seemed to have a seizure and fell to the ground. He was dead before the vet arrived; she thought he had suffered a stroke. We buried him in our field where he loved to run and play ball, and planted a cherry tree on top of him. Craig was more upset than I was; he had really grown to love Max, so for his birthday I bought him a puppy of the same breed.

Bica was also ageing, she was 16 years old, and still loved to swim with us, but she swam much slower than before; even I could keep up with her now and I couldn't help wondering if she would still be swimming with us next summer. Young Scratchy loved to swim, he was a natural and really fast. He would chase ducks and our resident heron when it dared to land on the river bank; the only birds that were safe were the kingfishers, they were much too fast for him. I had an old kayak that I took to rowing upriver with

Scratch so that I could keep up with him. Moppy would sit at the helm, and I would tie a piece of string to the front of the boat and throw it to Scratch, who would take it in his mouth and pull us along, his shoulders going up and down like little pistons and the tip of his tail always held above water, just like a rudder. Oh, how I loved that dog.

We called our new pup Lua Nova, which translates as New Moon, as she was totally black. Even at eight weeks old she was bigger than Moppy, and just as curly. She had a good pedigree so when she was old enough we decided to show her. It would be a new experience for me and I was quite excited about it. The day before the show, I took her to the parlour where she was shampooed and trimmed into the desired cut for showing.

I had done some research and knew that she would have the back third of her body and back legs shaved of hair. The front two thirds of her body were left long and curly except for her snout which would be shaved. I wasn't sure how I felt about this but if I wanted to enter a show with her, this cut would be expected. These days it is not so strict and some people show their dogs as they naturally are.

My research told me that this rather severe cut, originated from the days when the breed was used by Algarve fishermen to herd fish into their nets. The dogs were also expected to retrieve lost fishing tackle or nets, often diving down into the Atlantic sea. The hair around their body protected their vital organs from the cold water, but being shaved at the back end of their body, meant they could swim strongly in often rough conditions without being encumbered by heavy hair. It did make sense, but I still didn't like it.

Lua came first in her puppy class which we were thrilled about, but there was then a lot of waiting around until her second class. Portuguese water dogs are categorized as retrievers of fish, so she was in a mixed group of dogs which included Labradors and Spaniels. Lua lost sight of Steve and kept looking around for him. It was my stupid fault because I thought that if Steve went to stand behind the judges, and clicked his fingers at her, she would put her ears up and look pretty and alert. It backfired completely. She noticed that he was not in his seat, and became anxious; she wouldn't tune into me at all and just wanted to leave the ring and find her daddy! Well, if that was showing...I was done. Lua could become a farm dog instead.

CHAPTER 22

OLIVE HARVEST

When Craig had been a young boy, he loved to collect things. One year we visited a large festival where plastic beer cups were in abundance, littering the ground. He collected about 100 cups and took them home to plant seeds in. The seeds that he wanted to plant were from the loquat fruits that were plentiful in gardens at the time. We had been given a bucket full of the fruit by Francisco, the seeds were a very attractive glossy brown, almost like mini conkers, and each fruit had up to six seeds. Craig filled all of his newly acquired pots with soil and planted one seed in each pot. He carefully watered them all once; then promptly forgot about them.

A few months later, one seed germinated and started growing into a little nespereira tree, which is the Portuguese name for a loquat tree. We later planted it in our garden, and it is still there today. It has beautiful large, dark green ribbed leaves and has a delicious plum sized yellow fruit. The tree's umbrella shape and sweet smelling blossom make it a very attractive place to sit under for shade. It blossoms in early winter giving much needed nectar to insects and birds alike, but our area can be too cold for the newly pollinated fruits, and if we have a late frost, they will not survive and then we have no fruit to harvest the following summer.

Our kiwi vines on the other hand have gone wild. We originally planted them to give shade to the cottage patio; Steve built a framework for them to ramble over, but the plants gobbled it up within two years, their long tendrils reaching out for something bigger and higher to encompass. They give buckets full of fruit every winter which we all enjoy eating raw as they are high in vitamins, and the fruit stores well in a cool dark place.

One of my favourite fruit trees is our pomegranate. It has a pretty and long lasting blossom that is bright orange in colour, and when the fruit is ripe, I love to release the tiny red balls of deliciousness from the thick leathery skin, and add them to any salad dish as well as desserts.

We had always picked our olives, but as our riding business became more popular, we were often so busy at olive picking time, which is mid/end October, that we didn't have time for the labour-intensive task.

Francisco spotted our olive laden trees and couldn't believe that we were not picking them. When we told him that we didn't have time, he looked at us in exasperation. His eyes said it all; he would never understand his stupid foreign neighbours. He took Steve by the arm and led him down towards the olive tree, explaining in slow easy words.

"Olives are the fruit of the gods, not only are they good for our health but they are also good for our bank accounts." He rubbed his thumb and forefinger together to emphasise his point before continuing. "It is a crime to let them fall underfoot! If you are not going to pick them, can I?" He dodged around some fallen fruit—even they were of value to him.

"Yes, of course you can," said Steve, looking like a scolded child. "We don't like to see them wasted either, but we just don't have the time this year."

"I will come along with my family this afternoon" said Francisco happily, "and prune the trees for you at the same time."

That afternoon our yard was full of Francisco's family; even his young grandchildren helped, it was a true family operation. The family ox was hitched to a cart, and stood watching with doleful eyes as firstly they laid a big net on the ground around our two trees, then they bashed the branches with long sticks and the fruit rained down. Next, they lifted the four corners of the net, catching not only the olives, but leaves and sticks too.

Lourdes was Francisco's mother; she must have been at least 80 years old and had probably been olive harvesting for most of her life. Dressed in her normal black attire, she got down with difficulty onto the ground next to the net full of olives. I rushed to offer her a chair but she refused and asked me for a cushion instead as she needed to be on the ground. Then with deft fingers she and everyone else, young and old, sifted through the net of olives, picking out as many leaves and sticks as possible.

Next, all of the olives were tipped into large sacks and lifted onto the cart, along with the grandchildren. Francisco and his son-in-law pruned the two trees and loaded the branches, which still had a few stubborn olives attached, into the cart, and the ox pulled the whole lot home. Once the last few olives had been stripped, the branches and leaves would be fed to his goats. Nothing was wasted.

It was customary at this time, especially in the mountain villages, for a widow to dress in black for the rest of her life after her husband had died, as Lourdes did. This custom is slowly dying out, and although widows still dress in black, it is for a much shorter time span.

Craig had met a lovely girl at a festival in the Algarve, and after living in Lisbon for a while, they both moved in with us. I was so happy to have Craig back home, and Mariana was a charming girl, she was only 20 years old and spoke English perfectly. Portuguese people are generally dark haired and brown eyed, yet Mariana had very pretty blue eyes and lustrous strawberry blonde hair that tumbled almost to her bottom. She started helping Mella to improve her Portuguese language, and before long she had a list of foreign clients wanting to learn Portuguese from her.

Craig had trained as an electrician, but he was not enjoying the job. He and Mariana were looking into the possibility of becoming dog breeders; they would start small with just Lua as their founding female. Portuguese Water Dogs were becoming very fashionable, not only in Portugal but all over Europe and America. They contacted an established breeder who was happy to give them advice; Lua was two and a half years old which the breeder said was a good age. The breeder also owned a very handsome top class stud dog that would be the perfect father for Lua's pups. Craig and Mariana would need to take Lua to her stud farm for four days where her dog would mate with Lua daily when she was at her most receptive time.

The breeder believed in letting things happen naturally, so Lua and her dog were released in a large field to get to know each other first. Lua obviously fancied the male from the start, flirting and playing chase with him for about 15 minutes before finally coupling. Lua went to meet her mate on three more occasions before returning home for the long wait. She had a problem free pregnancy, and although she was huge, she stayed fit and healthy, and two months later, she gave birth to eight perfect little puppies.

Craig and Steve had made a big birthing box to keep the pups safe, and for the first two weeks, Lua didn't leave them for more than a few minutes. Craig and Mariana had a few sleepless nights as they wanted the birthing box to be in their room so that they could keep an eye on their little family day and night for the first week. But as the pups became more vocal, they had to move the box into another room so that they could get some sleep.

Oh, those puppies were such timewasters! I loved helping to weigh them regularly, to make sure they were all putting on weight. There were two little bruisers that were much bigger than the others, and a couple that were much smaller. I used to try to make sure that the little ones were latched on to the fullest teats a few times a day, and the bruisers were kept at bay for a bit. Once their eyes opened, they all became much more active, and then the trouble really started! Eight little pups would jump up at my legs each time I entered their room, biting at my trouser legs with their sharp little teeth, and undoing my laces.

Maia searched through her toy box for suitable toys to keep them amused. She found a large plastic fire engine that made noises and had a bell on the top. The pups loved it, the bravest ones climbed all over the car but every so often one pup would jump onto the bell and they would all fall off in astonishment, their little tails tucked between their legs, but it wasn't long before they were back for more fun. Some of them loved balls and some loved water, they were all developing their own special little personalities.

There had been a lot of interest in an advert that Craig had published on a Portuguese Waterdog website, and all too soon people were arriving to choose their puppies. An American family with Portuguese connections were holidaying in Lisbon and the whole family came to visit; because they couldn't choose which puppy they wanted, they bought two! They would be taking them to America with them as soon as they were old enough. An English lady bought two puppies, and another was sold locally, we kept our favourite little girl, and the last two pups would be living in the Algarve, which is where the breed originated from.

We could have sold them all twice over, so maybe this could be a lucrative business for Craig and Mariana; we had plenty of space on the farm and no neighbours to annoy. The puppies were all adorable, especially as we only had them for a short time and didn't have to cope with the teenage times. We called our little girl puppy Estrela, which means star, keeping the astrology theme. Most of the pups were black but Estrela had a white chest and white paws. Mariana had brought her own little dog with her, his name was Buddha. He was bigger than Moppy but smaller than Lua, and although he was a mixed breed dog, he had black curly hair and a very cute face, which made him look just like a half-grown Portuguese Waterdog. Counting Mella's spaniel Ray, we now had seven dogs on the farm.

We were expecting our last guests of the season, they were a mother, Kitty, and her grown up daughter Julia. Kitty was a true cockney; she was small and busty with wide expressive blue eyes and short blonde curly hair. Julia was tall and elegant and a very good rider. Kitty described her own riding style as "a clingon." She had never had a riding lesson in her life, but as a small child she had ridden her granddad's carthorse around the streets of London while he was collecting people's unwanted items. She remembered shouting out in her strong East End Cockney accent,

"Rag and Bone: bring out yer stuff!" as she sat high up on her granddad's cart.

She told us that she had loved his old piebald horse, and always kept her bread crusts for him. When her granddad became too old, she took over caring for the horse, and even remembered entering a small jumping competition on him. She hadn't won, but got a big round of applause for effort! I introduced Kitty to Domino who immediately smelt the minty polos that she had in her pocket and began frisking her.

"Aw, he's luvley, I luv 'is colour," she said turning to Julia, who had barely a hint of a cockney accent. Julia had been having riding lessons since she was a child and had already spotted Harrie. She asked me if she could ride him for the week, adding that she loved grey horses.

I enjoyed riding with them both, they were good fun, Kitty really screeched when she laughed but Domino didn't mind, they were well matched. We woke up one morning to pouring rain and a violent thunderstorm. Forked lightening lit up the still dark morning sky, I'm sure I could hear it hissing and cracking before the thunderous roar seemed to shake the very foundations of our house.

Kitty was very scared and was clinging on to Julia as they both came over from the cottage to have breakfast with us.

"Aw, gawd blimey, what a racket!" she said through chattering teeth, "I 'ope you're not expectin' me to ride in this?" But by the time we had all had breakfast, the sun was shining and the birds were singing. We set off on the horses in the washed air, there was no trace left now of the dusty paths of summer, but the ground was still warm, and a spooky grey mist enrobed the valleys, sending its tendrils upwards, before slowly dissipating into the warm sunshine.

How clear and beautiful the mountain looked; I felt as though I could reach out and touch its craggy peaks. The deciduous trees were dropping their splendid autumnal leaves of reds and burnt orange, and as we climbed higher the horses had to navigate their way over fallen leaves and torrents of water running down the steep tracks from the recent storm. We were making our way to our picnic ride which we called 'the ride to the top of the world'... I just hoped the storm didn't return!

It was a long climb for the horses but they were all fit, and the cooler weather made it easier for them. I was riding Guv and had often wondered which horse would be the fastest, Guv or Harrie? They were well matched in breeding and size so I knew it would be a close race. The mountain ridge track which led to the picnic spot was long and straight: it would be the perfect place to let the two horse's race. Julia excitedly told me that she had never raced at a flat out gallop before, but she was up for the challenge. Steve had agreed in advance to be at the finishing line to take a video, and as we came to the top of the hill and rounded a bend, we could see the ridge track spread out before us with a small stickman in the distance whom we assumed was him.

Guv and Harrie were both dancing on the spot, Domino and Kitty were plodding along behind. If I could have put a speech bubble on Domino it would have said something like:

"Don't expect me to join in your mad gallop; I will get there at my own pace and in my own time!"

As Guv and Harrie lurched into a flat-out gallop, I glanced over my shoulder to see Domino just breaking into a slow and steady canter. We were flying along the ridge track on the mountain top, my face was being whipped by Guv's long mane; a bird of prey circled above us as we raced neck and neck towards Steve. To be riding a Thoroughbred horse at breakneck speed along a mountain top....could life get much better? I fleetingly thought, as I glanced over at Julia; she had a look of exhilarated determination on her windswept face. Steve was getting closer, I could see the camera on us, and then he was gone. We flew past him, still neck and neck, I knew one of us would have to give in, so I started asking Guv to slow down, but he didn't want to, he wanted to win, just as he had when he was a young racehorse. Both horses had outstretched necks, their ears back and wide, blowing nostrils. I asked Guv again to slow down and this time he relented. I think it had suddenly occurred to him that he had passed his lunch spot! The horses liked this spot as much as we did because it was an abandoned goat farm that had a large grassy fenced area that they could graze while we ate our picnic food. We turned the horses around, and walked more sedately back to the grassy field. Domino was already there, having his saddle and bridle removed by Kitty.

"Slow and steady wins the race," I could imagine him saying as he collapsed into a well-deserved roll on the grass. Later we were examining the video footage taken by Steve, Julia and I both agreed that at the time we galloped past him, we were neck and neck, we were both winners! What made us all hoot with laughter was that after another minute, we heard the sound of hoof beats on the video, and as Steve panned around we saw Kitty and Domino wearily trotting up to the camera.

"I dunno 'ooze more knackered ... me or the 'orse!" she shrieked into the video camera.

Time passed quickly on the farm, and when Maia was 3 years old, we heard of a pony for sale that sounded just right for her. He was a Welsh section A crossed with Shetland. Mella, Maia and I went to visit the owner and view the pony, whose name was Misty. He was almost pure white; Maia ran towards him, and Mella just managed to grab her as we didn't know this pony at all.

"Don't worry," said the owner, "He's very used to small children, my two have outgrown him now, but they were only three and four years old when we bought him". Mella released Maia from her grip, and she hugged the pony, begging for someone to lift her on to his back. She spotted a plastic mounting block and was already dragging it over to Misty so that she could mount on her own.

Her favourite game at home was to put one of my saddles onto our mounting block and practise putting her foot into the stirrup and getting on and off. Another of her favourite games was to attach my long lunging rope around her waist, then she would ask me to lunge her in our arena, just as I would a horse. I had to shout "Walk! Trot! Canter!" to her, and scold her if she did the wrong strides. It was rather an embarrassing thing to have to try to explain to any Portuguese neighbours that passed by and saw us. They probably thought that all English people lunged their children!

Mella was just about light enough to ride Misty for a short while, so she set off for a trial ride with the owner riding another horse, and arrived back half an hour later. She was very impressed with Misty, saying that he didn't bat an eyelid when cars and trucks had passed him, or when two big dogs ran towards him. She had cantered him and found that he had good brakes. We decided to buy him but not just for Maia, she was told right from the start that he was a working pony, and would sometimes be used for young guests.

We added pictures of Misty to our website and almost immediately someone emailed to ask if they could come for a full board holiday with no riding for themselves, just some peace and quiet, while their two small children had riding lessons on Misty. Maia was in her element, she had two playmates for a week and could show them how to groom and feed Misty.

Maia had just learnt to trot and was keen to pass on her knowledge to her two playmates. Misty was not 100% reliable on the lunge line, and could sometimes be naughty with tiny tots, so poor Mella had to run beside him with a leading rein when he trotted, and of course as the children grew in confidence, all they wanted to do was trot! The children also loved to plait his mane; Misty's stable became known as 'the pony parlour' as the children plaited his mane with different colour braids each day, but he didn't mind a bit as long as his haynet was refilled regularly.

As Maia grew older, she became more and more attached to Domino. He was the type of horse that really wanted to communicate with humans. When Maia said in a high-pitched happy voice,

"Do you want a treat Dom?" he would nod his head furiously over the stable door until she produced his carrot, and if she didn't have any treats she would shake her head and say in a sad voice,

"Sorry Dom, no treats today," and he would shake his head over the stable door, as if he understood. Maia's latest game was to pick up a lightweight plastic mounting block and throw it over his stable door. Then she would climb over the door, and placing the mounting block close to him, she could climb up his leg, and somehow manage to get onto his back; there she would sit cuddling him and scratching his mane, which he loved and he would curl his upper lip in ecstasy. If ever Maia went missing, and Mella became anxious, I would just tell her to go and check Domino's stable and she was always there. One day Maia asked me if she could sleep with him in his stable, but I had to draw the line at that!

My friend Jan, loaned me a vaulting surcingle which is a wide leather padded strap that goes around the girth of the horse. It has three leather handles on top. Domino was exceptionally good on the lunge and very comfortable to ride bareback, so I started offering lessons to my guests in bareback riding. It is the very best way to improve your riding position and the handles on the vaulting surcingle gave extra security. Bess, who was one of my regular students, wanted to learn to vault properly, so with some help from my friend Jan who had loaned me the surcingle, and had taught vaulting in the past, we started practising.

"To be a good equestrian vaulter, you need to be a gymnast first." Jan told us. Bess was tall, young and agile, but she hadn't had a lot of gymnastic training so it wasn't easy for her, but she persevered and before long, she was able to run next to Domino's inside shoulder as he cantered on the lunge, then taking one of the handles on the surcingle, she leapt up onto his back as he was still cantering round. It is much harder than it sounds, I can assure you.

Maia loved to watch, and when the lesson finished, I would allow her to sit up on Domino, holding on to the handles, and before long she was trotting and cantering bareback on the lunge line, even though her tiny legs only just reached across his back. She was a natural rider with amazing balance, and not even four years old! I wondered what the future would hold for her.

Mella and Simon had bought a house about 5 kilometres from us and they would soon be moving away from our farm. At the same time, Craig and Mariana had rented a house nearby and they too would be moving soon. Our farm, that had been alive with our noisy family for so long, would become much more tranquil. I think Steve was happy with the thought of having some peace and quiet, but I was not so sure about me. I loved the bustle of family life, the drama, the laughter; the tears! But I knew that they would all be visiting regularly, probably too regularly! Perhaps we needed a new adventure, and one was already forming in our minds. However, it would not coalesce yet, as there is *One More Slice of Paradise* still to come........

In the third and final chapter of my trilogy, we meet new horses as Guv, Smartie, and Roxy retire from riding, and we meet many new guests, nice and not so nice! We buy our first campervan called 'The Big Red Love Bus', and two more beautiful grandchildren are born, Arli and Nala.

I am always happy to receive emails at. *sandracross421@gmail.com*

I am also on Facebook, where I am constantly uploading photos of the animals that you have met in my books.

https://www.facebook.com/SandraCross421

Sandra Cross, Author of *Paradise*.

Printed in Great Britain
by Amazon

20928568R00120